Swedenborg's
GARDEN *of*
THEOLOGY

Swedenborg's
GARDEN *of*
THEOLOGY

❦

An INTRODUCTION *to*
Emanuel Swedenborg's Published Theological Works

JONATHAN S. ROSE

SWEDENBORG FOUNDATION PRESS
West Chester, Pennsylvania

Originally published in 2005 in *Emanuel Swedenborg: Essays for the New Century Edition on His Life, Work, and Impact*, ed. Jonathan S. Rose et al.

Library of Congress Cataloging-in-Publication Data

Rose, Jonathan S.
    Swedenborg's garden of theology : an introduction to Swedenborg's published theological works / Jonathan S. Rose.
        p. cm.
    ISBN 978-0-87785-333-6 (alk. paper)
1. Swedenborg, Emanuel, 1688-1772. I. Title.
BX8711.R67 2010
230'.94—dc22
          2009049141

The author is grateful for the editorial help and suggestions received from Morgan L. Beard, Alicia L. Dole, Kristin King, Luken Potts, and Stuart Shotwell

Cover and interior design by Karen Connor
Cover image: Design for a botanic garden, from "Hints on the Formation of Gardens and Pleasure Grounds" by John Claudius Loudon (1783–1843) published 1812 (color litho) by English School (19th century).
Image courtesy of The Stapleton Collection and The Bridgeman Art Library.

Manufactured in the United States of America

Swedenborg Foundation
320 North Church Street
West Chester, PA 19380
www.swedenborg.com

Contents

	Introduction	vii
One	The Gateway: Swedenborg's Claim	3
Two	The Layout *of the* Garden *of* Swedenborg's Theological Works	7
Three	The Population *of the* Garden	19
Four	Problematic Content	39
Five	Unusual Specimens *and the* Doorway *to the* Mirror Garden	43
Six	The Style *of* Swedenborg's Published Theological Works	53
Seven	Swedenborg's Invitation	65
	Appendix: Theological Works Published by Emanuel Swedenborg	67
	Notes	73
	Bibliography	93

Introduction

In 1743, in the heart of the Enlightenment and in the middle of his life, a European scientist by the name of Emanuel Swedenborg (1688–1772) underwent a spiritual crisis and personal transformation. He had been abroad for several years on one of his many journeys, but now returned home to his native Sweden, where he had recently acquired property near Stockholm—an unassuming plot of land, about 1.2 acres (0.5 hectares) on Södermalm, an island just south of the city. He had never owned a home before. Though he had inherited a share in his family's Starbo iron works and other mining properties, during his adult life he generally lived in rented quarters, an arrangement made simpler by his lifelong bachelorhood. This new purchase was destined to become a showcase garden.

Sometime over the following decade, Swedenborg had contractors enclose the entire plot with a high wooden fence. A second fence divided the eastern third of the land, which held the main buildings, from the rest, which was to be dedicated to plantings. A pathway east to west and another south to north divided the rectangular garden into four equal areas. These quadrants, although their plantings no doubt changed over time, seem generally to have been dedicated each to a different type of vegetation: trees valued for their edible fruit, trees valued for other reasons, smaller plants valued for their fruits and vegetables, and smaller plants valued for their flowers.

Within his garden's large-scale order and symmetry Swedenborg put many strange and wonderful things. The gate into the garden was a massive, highly ornate, baroque French archway, very much out of place among the simple Swedish buildings and fences. The vegetation ranged from the ordinary—such as carrots, spinach, and cucumbers—to the foreign and exotic, such as blue roses; shaped boxwoods from Holland; dogwoods, mulberries, and sweet corn from Pennsylvania; and roses and melons from Africa. In one spot was a large suspended cage for exotic birds; in another a door in the fence seemed as if it must lead to a second garden, but instead opened onto a set of mirrors reflecting the real garden behind the viewer. Toward the southwest corner, by the rose gardens, Swedenborg had his workers construct a virtually inescapable maze formed of boards, intended for the amusement of his many visitors.[1]

Equally noteworthy was the pretty and diminutive summerhouse with a full view of the garden. It held little more than a writing desk. Here, in this modest house, Swedenborg often labored over the theological works for which he is now best known.

These theological volumes were the product of more than two decades of labor. When first printed, they comprised eighteen separate and quite distinctive works in twenty-five quarto volumes totaling about three and a half million words—researched, composed, published, and (for the most part) distributed by Swedenborg himself. Although they appear to be aimed at different audiences, they heavily cross-reference each other and can be seen as a unified whole.

In a number of ways Swedenborg's theological works resemble his garden. Viewed in general terms, they display symmetry and balance, method and sequence. Their approach is varied, their scope comprehensive. In them one senses the author's intelligent yet humble reverence for the peace that order brings. As Swedenborg's garden had large-scale symmetry both east to west and south to north, his theology shows horizontal symmetries of love and wisdom, will and intellect, good and truth, goodwill and faith; and vertical symmetries of the Lord and humankind, heaven and hell, heaven and earth, spirit and body, and the inner and outer levels of the mind. Although twenty-two years passed between publication of the first and the last title, the theology of the eighteen works is extremely coherent and consistent. Viewed more narrowly, however, Swedenborg's published theological works—again, like his garden—contain many elements that excite bafflement, wonder, or delight.

This book is an invitation to the reader to enter the garden of Swedenborg's works, and to look at them from both the long and the close perspective.

Swedenborg's
GARDEN *of*
THEOLOGY

ONE

The Gateway: Swedenborg's Claim

> I realize many will claim that no one can talk to
> spirits and angels as long as bodily life continues,
> or that I am hallucinating, or that I have circulated
> such stories in order to play on people's credulity,
> and so on. But none of this worries me; I have seen,
> I have heard, I have felt.[1]—*Secrets of Heaven* §68

The gateway to Swedenborg's theological garden lies in understanding his unique claim to spiritual experience. The first chapter of the first of his published theological works closes with a bold claim of his direct experience of the spiritual realm: *Vidi, audivi, sensi*, "I have seen, I have heard, I have felt." His phrase is a conscious echo of Julius Caesar's terse encapsulation of a great victory: *Veni, vidi, vici*, "I came, I saw, I conquered." Unlike Caesar, though, Swedenborg is proclaiming conquest not of a foe, but of the uncertainties that vitiate so much human experience of the spiritual realm. He asserts that another world exists: he has seen it, heard it, felt it.

Swedenborg had ample credentials in European society and in his scientific career. He was born the son of a high-ranking Lutheran cleric and educated at Uppsala, the most prestigious university in seventeenth-century Scandinavia. He held a seat in the Swedish House of Nobles as head of his family, which was ennobled in 1719. He undertook extensive research in fields ranging from earth science to anatomy, and he earned an international reputation as a scientist. With this noteworthy career behind him, and conscious of his status in European society, when he turned to theology after his spiritual crisis he could not help being acutely aware of his lack of credentials as a theologian.[2] Thus the importance of his claim: it constitutes his authority to share the spiritual insights he felt compelled (even divinely commanded) to publish to humankind.

He is of course not alone in claiming experience of this other world. It has many names: paradise, eternity, the world beyond the grave, the hereafter, the spirit world. Many have reportedly journeyed there in meditation, in near-death or other transcendental experiences, or in dreams. Many of these reported experiences are not bodily. Travelers to this realm leave the body inactive behind them, and some even report seeing the physical self from a distance. To the skeptical, claims of such nonbodily experiences certainly seem enough to strain belief; but Swedenborg claimed even more. He asserted that from his mid-fifties through the rest of his life he lived and functioned in both the material and the spiritual world at once.[3] He could maintain an awareness of another world with all his senses, carrying on conversations with its inhabitants, beholding its nature and structure, while nevertheless pursuing a wide range of activities in this world, from publishing to gardening, from socializing to being active in politics.

Some critics have indeed labeled him mentally ill or insane for his claim. Contemporary reports, however, attest that he was intelligent, clear-headed, reliable, and kind. There is abundant documentary evidence that he was physically, politically, and intellectually active until his death at eighty-four. If this was insanity, it was an illness strangely beneficial.[4]

There is also independent evidence, reported by multiple witnesses, that supports Swedenborg's claim to be in contact with angels and spirits, although as proof it is not incontestable. Three incidents in particular caused a stir in his lifetime, drawing the attention and commentary even of the philosopher Immanuel Kant (1724–1804), who discussed them in a letter to an acquaintance.[5] In brief, they are as follows:

1. While on a visit to the Swedish city of Göteborg, Swedenborg clairvoyantly saw and accurately reported details of a fire simultaneously raging 250 miles away in Stockholm.

2. He helped a widow find a receipt for a substantial sum that a silversmith claimed her husband had never paid, though only the deceased husband could have known its location.

3. In response to a challenge, he confounded Queen Lovisa Ulrika of Sweden (1720–82) by telling her a family secret that she declared no living person could have revealed to him.[6]

Although he himself did not record these incidents, he attested to their accuracy, maintaining they were evidence that he was in contact with angels and spirits.[7] Both at the time and since, people have found these and several other independently recorded anecdotes convincing testimonies to the veracity of Swedenborg's larger claim.[8]

The Layout of the Garden
of Swedenborg's Theological Works

If a curious visitor steps through the gateway, the overall layout of the garden of the eighteen works becomes visible. In this theological garden, Swedenborg presents a Christian message, but one that is distinct from other forms of Christianity. Its core teachings, terms, and phrases recur consistently throughout, surrounded by an unending variety of illustrative and experiential material. If he had used his spiritual experiences alone as the foundation of his theology, the structure would stand on something relatively unprovable, requiring a leap of faith on the reader's part. However, he makes extensive use of objective foundations as well, including logic, established empirical knowledge, and Scripture (which as a devout Christian he considers an objectively sound authority). He employs deductive argumentation, draws analogies to physical and social realities, quotes the Bible, and recounts and comments on his spiritual experiences to support a comprehensive theology whose layout can be summarized as follows.

GOD AND HUMANITY, AND THE HUMANITY OF GOD

In Swedenborg's theology, there is one God, who is generally called "the Lord" (Latin *Dominus,* a title rather than a name, meaning "the one in charge"). The Lord is human, and therefore all creation to a greater or lesser degree reflects humanity. Central to Swedenborg's theology is an identification of Jesus, a human being, with God, the infinite source of creation. However, Swedenborg seems stringently to avoid any indication of masculine or feminine gender in God. He consistently uses the term *homo,* "a human," rather than a gendered term for God's humanity; and where he uses other terms for God, such as "the Infinite," "the Divine," or "the Divine Human," he casts them as neuter rather than feminine or masculine.

To be human is to possess heart and mind, or, in other words, will or volition and intellect or discernment. The will or volition is the faculty that enables human beings to experience purposefulness, values, intent, love, and emotion, while the intellect or discernment enables the experience of wisdom, intelligence, reflection, and thought. The human body is "merely an obedient servant" (*True Christianity* 397), doing what the will intends and saying what the intellect thinks. To be human, then, is to have a spirit or mind composed of will and intellect that lives in the spiritual world, and a body composed of flesh and blood that lives in the material world or physical realm. The spirit possesses feeling, thought, and awareness; it also enlivens the body's sensation, speech, and movement.

Love is the essence and source of human life. There are four overarching categories of love: love for the Lord, love for our neighbor, love for things of the world, and love for ourselves. The former two are good loves. The latter two are good unless they predominate over the former, in which case they become evil (*Divine Love and Wisdom* 396). Love for the Lord is the highest of the loves, and is opposite to love for ourselves, the lowest love. Each of these loves has derivative feelings or desires, like the branches of a tree, and attendant thoughts and knowledge. Everyone is in essence his or her own ruling love—the soul, a person's inner being, is composed of that love, a love unique to each individual. Nonetheless, all humans experience loves that can be grouped under the four overarching categories.

Perfect humanity characterizes the Lord. The Lord's essence is pure love and pure wisdom, an infinite love that intends the salvation of every human being, and an infinite wisdom that sees what laws and structure the universe must have to achieve this intent. Divine love and divine wisdom are utterly united. We ourselves divide them into two in our thinking, just as we generally conceive of the sun's light and heat as two different things when in fact they are the same energy (*True Christianity* 41).

The object of the Lord's love, the overall purpose in creating and sustaining the universe, is to populate a heaven with human beings whom the Lord loves and who love the Lord freely in return.[1] Central to the Lord's plan is human spiritual freedom, meaning the individual's ability to choose between good and evil loves, and between true and false thoughts. Until their choice of heaven or hell is complete, human beings remain in a balance between good and evil, and between truth and falsity, so that their choice will be free and deliberate.

In the beginning God created two worlds, the spiritual and the physical. These two worlds are related through what Swedenborg calls correspondences. For example, just as there is a sun seen high above our world, there is a sun seen high above the spiritual world; but the sun in the spiritual world consists of pure love, whereas the sun in the physical world consists of pure fire. In essence and substance, they are fundamentally different, but in form and function they play parallel roles in their respective worlds.

The spiritual world is more real than the physical world. Composed of spiritual substance, it shares nothing in common with physical reality. Yet although these two worlds are discrete, the human mind senses and perceives them as being similar. In many places throughout his writings, Swedenborg describes people in the spiritual world who do not realize they have died, or who are amazed to find themselves after death in a world so much like the one they left (see, for example, *True Christianity* 80:4 and 160:3, 7, and *Marriage Love* 182:7). Human beings living in the physical world form a necessary bridge between the two worlds, having minds in the spiritual world and bodies in the physical world. From creation, human beings were intended to live consciously in both worlds at once, sensing spiritual reality with the senses of their spirit and physical reality with the senses of their body (*Secrets of Heaven* 69).

Because the Lord is human, heaven reflects humanity, and does so at multiple levels. Taken together, the whole of the heavens reflects a single human form; Swedenborg terms this aggregate human form the "Universal Human" or "Grand Man." Yet each of its component parts—its two kingdoms and three heavens—is by itself a complete human form. On even smaller scales, each community in heaven is also in the human form, as is each angel (*Heaven and Hell* 51–77). By "human form," Swedenborg is not referring to the physical shape of a human body but rather to the complex functional interaction of components, both mental and physical, that comprise a human being. Swedenborg even goes so far as to say that everything good and true is in the human form (*Heaven and Hell* 460).

On whatever level, then, and on however wide or narrow a scope, there is wholeness and humanity. As the ancients implied with their concept of a human being as a microcosm, each individual has a whole heaven and a whole world within.[2]

Swedenborg presents both men and women as complete human beings because each has will and intellect. However, he assigns specific characteristics to each gender. In some passages from his books, the essential distinction between female and male is that will and love predominate in women, while wisdom and intellect are dominant in men (*Heaven and Hell* 369; see also *Marriage Love* 33, 91, 160, 187, 218:2, 296:1). He expands on this in *Marriage Love,* where he describes men as being inwardly forms of love but outwardly forms of wisdom, while women are inwardly forms of wisdom but outwardly forms of love (§32). This gives the genders different abilities and forms of wisdom (*Marriage Love* 168, 174–6).

In another title, though, the association is reversed: women are related to wisdom and men to love (*True Christianity* 37:3, 41:3). One passage suggests that in what Swedenborg calls the heavenly or celestial kingdom of heaven, love corresponds to the male and wisdom corresponds to the female; in the lower, spiritual kingdom of heaven, however, the opposite obtains: love corresponds to the female and wisdom to the male (*Secrets of Heaven* 8994:4).

Swedenborg's gender distinctions notwithstanding, his works generally emphasize the similarities between male and female much more than their differences, in that his theology is usually expressed in universal terms and concerns both sexes equally. Only in his work on marriage are the sexes treated separately in any sustained way. The generic Latin term *homo*, "human being," occurs approximately 28,300 times in Swedenborg's published theological works—far more than the approximately 6,100 combined instances of gendered terms such as *vir*, "man" or "husband"; *femina*, "woman"; *mulier*, "woman"; and *uxor*, "wife."

The Meaning of Heaven and Hell

In the spiritual world, the Lord is but rarely experienced with the senses in human form. He might appear in heaven or on earth by filling an angel with his presence, but in heaven it is far more common for angels to see the Lord as a sun far above. His love and truth shower the spiritual world much the way the heat and light of our sun shower the earth, but while our sun is only one of many stars, the Lord is the only sun of the spiritual world. As mentioned above, rather than being made of "pure fire" like our sun, the sun of heaven is pure love (*Revelation Unveiled* 468).[3]

The spiritual world comprises heaven and hell, and between the two is what Swedenborg calls the world of spirits. People who have turned toward God and practiced goodwill toward their neighbor have become a heaven in miniature, so to speak, during life in this world, and will live in heaven after death. People who have turned toward themselves and the world to the exclusion of God and their neighbor have become a hell in miniature here, and will live in hell after death. The world of spirits, with heaven above and hell below, is a temporary home to all those who have died but are not yet in either heaven or hell (*Heaven and Hell* 421–22). The world of spirits is also a temporary home to the human mind while the body remains alive in the physical world, although people on earth are generally unaware of the world of spirits, because their spiritual senses are usually closed.

Heaven and hell are separate and opposite. Although inhabitants of hell are free to visit heaven, without special protection they find they cannot breathe properly there and suffer severe distress until they return home. Neither can angels breathe in hell unless they are granted special protection. All inhabitants of heaven (called angels), all inhabitants of the world of spirits (called spirits, angelic spirits, and evil spirits), and all inhabitants of hell (called satans, devils, demons, and evil spirits) were once human beings living in the physical world, whether on this earth or on some other planet. There is but one universal human race.

The human mind has three levels: a lowest or earthly plane, a middle or spiritual plane, and a highest or heavenly plane. At birth these levels are neither open nor closed. These levels exist in potential form at birth, and they open or close as a person grows and makes choices. The three levels of the mind answer to three levels of willingness to follow the Lord. Swedenborg writes that willingness to follow the Lord is a form of innocence—not the innocence of childhood, but a wise innocence like that of the angels (*Heaven and Hell* 276–83). To follow the Lord with no more than bodily obedience opens our minds at the lowest level and prepares us for life in the lowest heaven; to follow with intelligence as well opens our minds at the middle level and prepares us to live in the middle heaven; and to follow with love opens our minds at the highest level and prepares us to live in the highest heaven (see *Secrets of Heaven* 9594). The amount of openness is something we choose and allow ourselves. To turn away from the

Lord and heaven toward an exclusive focus on ourselves and the things of the world closes our minds to heavenly influence from above and opens them to hellish influence from below, again to different levels depending on the depth and intensity of our participation in evil. The higher levels of the mind close, and the spirit becomes merely earthly; or worse yet, sense-oriented; or worst of all, flesh-oriented.

INFLOW AND THE INDIVIDUAL

The Lord is present in time and space, but is not subject to their limitations. Omnipresent, the Lord flows directly into heaven; into the world of spirits; into hell; into the human mind; and into animals, plants, and inanimate objects, in the same way on the largest and smallest imaginable scales (see *Divine Love and Wisdom* 77–82). At the same time, there is also a hierarchy of inflow (also called influx). Good and truth from the Lord cascade through the higher and lower heavens, passing through angelic spirits in the world of spirits into the higher levels of the human mind; while evil and falsity, which are simply twisted echoes of that same inflowing life from above, then rise up from the lower to the higher hells, passing through evil spirits in the world of spirits into the lower levels of the human mind. While we are alive in this world, then, all our thoughts and perceptions, whether true or false, and all our emotions, values, and desires, whether good or evil, flow in from God through various parts of the other world. This inflow creates the balance between good and evil in which we are kept until we finally choose heaven or hell (*Heaven and Hell* 589–600).

Swedenborg sees the universe as responding to the direct and indirect inflow of the Lord's life in an unlimited variety of ways. He draws an analogy to sunlight, which flows out as one thing but seems to change according to its reception, occasioning beautiful colors and aromas when it shines on flowers, for example, but disgusting colors and odors when it shines on excrement (*Heaven and Hell* 569; *Divine Love and Wisdom* 348). Like all things in nature, human beings are vessels formed to receive life rather than life-forms in their own right. Unlike flowers and excrement, human beings have a range of choices in their response to the life that inflows from the Lord. Swedenborg urges us to welcome the good that flows in by attributing it to the Lord and reject the evil by sending it back to hell:

> If we believed the way things really are, that everything good comes from [the Lord] and everything evil from hell, then we would not take credit for the good within us or blame for the evil. Whenever we thought or did anything good, we would focus on the Lord, and any evil that flowed in we would throw back into the hell it came from. But since we do not believe in any inflow from heaven or from hell and therefore believe that everything we think and intend is in us and from us, we make the evil our own and defile the good with our feeling that we deserve it.[4]

By design, we cannot escape the appearance that we live on our own. What Swedenborg calls our sense of autonomy is a gift from the Lord that makes reciprocation and salvation possible. Therefore the intellectual belief and recognition that good and evil flow in will be repeatedly undermined by the experience of being alive, of apparently possessing our own feelings, thoughts, and sensations.

To progress spiritually, then, requires both a recognition and an action. We need to recognize intellectually that everything good and evil flows in, and yet we need to act with all our apparent power and life to stop doing what is evil and start doing what is good. To acknowledge the Lord and not to take action is to remain where we began; to take action and not to acknowledge the Lord is to overinflate the self.

Our seemingly autonomous action and the recognition of our debt to the Lord appear in a five-point summary of what to believe and how to live:

1. There is one God; the divine trinity exists within him; and he is the Lord God the Savior Jesus Christ.
2. Believing in him is a faith that saves.
3. We must not do things that are evil—they belong to the Devil and come from the Devil (by which Sweden-borg means hell in general).
4. We must do things that are good—they belong to God and come from God.
5. We must do these things as if we did them ourselves, but we must believe that they come from the Lord working with us and through us.[5]

Swedenborg's concept of apparent self-life leads to an unusual picture of what happens to the self in the course of spiritual progress. He emphasizes the uniqueness of all individuals even before they regenerate, or undergo a process of spiritual rebirth (*Heaven and Hell* 486; *Divine Love and Wisdom* 318; *Marriage*

Love 186:2). As people then regenerate, rather than losing self and merging with the Divine, the closer they get to the Lord the more distinctly they feel like themselves and feel free (*Divine Providence* 42–44). Although heaven consists of countless communities, the best angels of all live on their own (*Heaven and Hell* 50), perhaps because they have become increasingly differentiated from others as they have drawn closer to the Lord.

THREE

The Population of the Garden

ust as Swedenborg's garden comprised a wide variety of both common and exotic plants, his theological garden encompasses the varied spiritual forms taken by the human race in the past. According to Swedenborg, at any time throughout human history on this planet only one of the many existing religions carried the primary responsibility for connecting heaven and earth. His theology is unusual in that it teaches that a variety of religions is necessary because only multiple religions can provide important diversity (*Divine Providence* 326:10) and lead a variety of peoples to salvation (*Heaven and Hell* 318–19; *Divine Providence* 253–54, 325–26, and 330:5, 6). Yet for the sake of heaven's connection to earth, there has been at any given time a single monotheistic religion at the spiritual center, so to speak. Although different religions with different forms of revelation have played this central role at different times in history, Swedenborg calls them all *ecclesiae* or "churches" (even though that term originally had a strictly Christian connotation). Many readers of Swedenborg feel that as humanness is universal on scales both large and small, the qualities of each of the churches discussed below reflect aspects of the individual; thus ecclesiastical history can also be taken personally. Swedenborg refers to each church's revelation as "the Word," although he more commonly uses that term to refer to the Bible, or such parts of it as he recognizes as having an inner meaning.[1]

The Early Churches

In the beginning there was the Golden Age, also called the earliest or most ancient church. Human beings responded to the Lord with their hearts and allowed the Lord to open their minds at the highest or heavenly level. As a result there was open communication between those living on earth and those in heaven. People saw the Lord as the only source of humanity and by contrast would not call themselves human. The will and intellect were so united that whatever people loved they thought about and did. There was no loop of objectivity in the intellect to second-guess the desires of the heart. At first no such objectivity was needed, because what their hearts desired was good. Marriages were strong and deeply spiritual in earliest times (*Marriage Love* 75). By means of correspondences, people saw heavenly qualities reflected in the trees, plants, and animals around them, as well as in each other and in the events of their lives. Having no spoken or written language, and needing none, they received direct revelation and guidance from God through the mirror of nature, through dreams and visions, and through their contact with angels.

In time, however, the human race fell. People turned away from the Lord and heaven to set their primary focus on themselves and the world. No longer wanting to be receivers and containers of life from God, people wished to be life-forms in themselves. This development, symbolized by the Flood in Genesis, caused evil desires and twisted thinking to inundate their minds, to the point that they passed beyond salvability. They "drowned" in their inability to separate thought from desire. Although they retained the indestructible quality known as the *likeness* of God—meaning life, awareness, creative power, and immortality—they were no longer in the *image* of God, no longer godly. Life became a spiritual death. That age, then, passed from the light side to the dark side of living from the heart.

The Lord restored freedom and the possibility of salvation to the human race by making the intellect separable from the will. The intellect gained the ability to rise at times above the tide of evil in the will so that it could see what is true and what would be good. The sight of truth could then redirect thoughts and behavior toward a new will, a second nature that was loving and heavenly.

The alteration of the human mind began the Silver Age, which Swedenborg calls the early or ancient church, a collection of diverse religious groups widely spread around the eastern Mediterranean Sea.[2] People then were centered in the intellect rather than the heart and needed written revelation to communicate with heaven. Their revelation, the ancient or early Word, now lost, contained profoundly allegorical tales and obscure prophecies of the Messiah to come. They imbibed it intellectually, which led to a communication with heaven, but a poorer one than the Golden Age had enjoyed. Swedenborg labels them spiritual rather than heavenly. In time, just as the earliest people had fallen from their golden state, the people of the Silver Age lapsed into worshiping idols and using their knowledge of correspondences to do evil, in some cases in the form of black magic.

To ensure protection from evil the Lord then took away spiritual knowledge altogether, providing instead written instructions in the Pentateuch in the Bible (Genesis, Exodus, Leviticus,

Numbers, and Deuteronomy) for rituals and practices that would link heaven and earth obliquely. Conscious contact of the mind or heart with heaven was lost. The Copper and Iron ages—the Hebrew, the Israelite, and the Jewish churches respectively[3]—were neither heavenly nor spiritual, Swedenborg claims; he labels them earthly, and even sense-oriented and flesh-oriented. As marriage and religion go hand in hand, the marriages of that time were not spiritual either (*Marriage Love* 78). Swedenborg asserts that people at that time followed God in a bodily way, obeying instructions written in Scripture.[4]

The Christian Church

In time people rebelled against even this lowest form of adherence, making it necessary for the ancient prophecies to be fulfilled. God ("Jehovah,"[5] "the Father," or "the Divine") conceived in Mary's womb the child Jesus (the "Son" or "the Human"), whose soul was divine but whose lower mind was riddled with accumulated hereditary evil. Though God had always been *spiritually* human, in Jesus God became *physically* human.[6] Referring to Jesus, Swedenborg gives the following as "the faith of the new heaven and the new church in universal form":

> The Lord from eternity, who is Jehovah, came into the world to gain control over the hells and to glorify his own human nature; without this, not one mortal could have been saved; those who believe in him are saved. (*True Christianity* 2)

While alive on earth, Jesus underwent something parallel to the process of repentance, reformation, and regeneration that everyone must go through to be united to God and heaven. For ordinary human beings, the process involves examining oneself, recognizing and acknowledging evil of actions or even of thought and desire, praying for help, and beginning a new life. Doing so leads at times to inner battles between good and evil; our higher or inner self is in conflict with our lower or outer self. These are called crises or temptations and occasion great psychological pain, but they also enhance spiritual freedom of choice. If we fight against the evil habit or inclination with apparent autonomy, yet acknowledge the Lord's power and our own true helplessness, the Lord pushes the evil to the periphery and clears a larger channel for love to flow through. Numerous battles over a lifetime bring us from a selfish, hellish state to a loving, heavenly one.

Jesus's battles were comparable, though on an infinite scale, and though divinity rather than heavenliness was the desired outcome. From early childhood he was under continual attack by every devil and satan in hell. Over the course of his life on earth he conquered all the hells and brought them under his dominion, restored freedom to heaven and the world of spirits, and glorified or transformed his human nature, which means that he made it divine.[7] His suffering and dying on the cross completed the process of glorification. The unknowable Divine had become picturable and knowable in Jesus Christ.

Although states of apparently separate consciousness in Jesus cause the appearance of a duality or trinity of persons in the New Testament (such as when, for example, he calls on, prays to, or even feels forsaken by his "Father"), there was never more than one person of God. There is a trinity in the Lord, but a trinity like that of the spirit, the body, and the actions of an individual

(*The Lord* 46). One person includes the three aspects known as
Father, Son, and Holy Spirit. Swedenborg summarizes this most
briefly as follows: "There is one God; the divine trinity exists
within him; and he is the Lord God the Savior Jesus Christ"
(*True Christianity* 3).

One of the reasons Jesus came to earth was to begin a new
church. Like the churches that preceded, Christianity was char-
acterized by initial purity and clarity. According to Swedenborg,
early Christians focused on worshiping the Lord, repenting
of evil, and loving others. However, by the time of the Nicene
Council in 325, that purity and clarity were already lost, as evil
and falsity took hold of the Christian church. Roman Catholicism fell into believing in a trinity of persons, adoring Mary and
the saints, and withholding Scripture and the wine of communion from the laity. In Swedenborg's view, though, Catholicism's
great error was to attribute to the pope and the ecclesiastical
hierarchy the power to open and shut heaven, which belongs to
the Lord alone.

According to Swedenborg, the Protestant Reformation led
to a new church that corrected many of Catholicism's errors.
The greater study of Scripture increased the amount of spiritual
light in the world (see *True Christianity* 270). The Protestant or
Reformed churches, however, fell into the error of seeing Jesus's
divine and human natures as separate and asserting that we are
"justified" or deemed righteous and saved on the basis of our
faith alone. Swedenborg briefly but repeatedly charges that the
Reformed church split God into three and the Lord into two,
and separated faith from love and goodwill (*Revelation Unveiled*
263, 294:6, 481, 537, 550; *Survey* 88). Protestantism's study of
the Bible brought no correction to the doctrine of the Trinity;

and its doctrine of salvation by faith alone induced complete spiritual darkness.

Swedenborg says that every church follows a certain pattern: it rises, it falls, and it comes to an end in a last judgment. The end of the first church was symbolized by the Flood (Genesis 7 and 8). The other pre-Christian churches came to their last judgment at the time of Christ's coming. The Book of Revelation in its spiritual meaning predicts the last judgment on Catholicism and Protestantism as churches, and also the coming of a new church symbolized by the New Jerusalem. These last judgments were spiritual rather than physical. They all occurred in the spiritual world and primarily affected its inhabitants. However, they also had an impact on the mental condition and spiritual freedom of people still alive in the physical world, because the mind is spiritual. The long-standing expectation of a last judgment on earth, a cataclysmic change in the political and physical arenas of this world, is the result of Christianity taking Scripture too literally, after its heart and life had turned away from God. Swedenborg frequently criticizes this belief in a physical last judgment, saying that such ludicrous ideas undermine more important beliefs in the Lord and the Word (*Heaven and Hell* 312).

THE NEW CHURCH

Swedenborg presents himself, then, as writing at a dramatic and even crucial point in human spiritual history. He claims to have witnessed the last judgment on the Catholic and Protestant churches—the last judgment predicted in Matthew and in the Book of Revelation—in the spiritual world when the Christian calendar read 1757.[8] The entire sequence of the ages had been enacted, from Golden, Silver, Copper, and Iron to Iron

Mixed with Clay, which was the Christian church.[9] Although the solstice of divine absence had passed with the birth of Christ seventeen hundred years earlier, and ever since then a greater light had become available to the world, nevertheless a winter of evil and falsity had increased to the point that at Swedenborg's day "a total damnation stood at the door and threatened" (*True Christianity* 3, 121, 579). Swedenborg reports that during his own lifetime the most recent church, Protestantism, had become spiritually defunct (see *True Christianity* 760–62). As its leaders and followers died, many of them were bringing unrepentant lives and twisted impressions of Scripture and theology into the world of spirits, from which they influenced those still on earth. Hell was on the verge of winning the struggle for every human soul.

By his own testimony, Swedenborg was given consciousness of the spiritual world to witness the Last Judgment of 1757 and to facilitate the Lord's Second Coming[10] and the establishment of a new church. Many of the eighteen titles of Swedenborg's published theological works present themselves as teachings for this new church, the New Jerusalem.[11] In contrast to many millenarians of his age, Swedenborg maintains that the Last Judgment will have virtually no immediate political or social effect on earth (*Last Judgment* 73). Although he implies that the new church will last forever (*True Christianity* 791), he predicts that at first it will grow slowly (*Revelation Unveiled* 546–47), that the spiritual meaning of the Word will not be recognized for "a long time" (*Sacred Scripture* 25), and that "a time, times, and half a time" (a reference to Daniel 12:7 and Revelation 12:14) will pass before these teachings will be well received on earth (*Marriage Love* 533). He also predicts, however, that the Lord will eventually restore marriage to a spiritual form like that of the ancient church, and draw the new church into a closer relationship with the Lord and a greater affiliation with angels than any previous church had enjoyed.[12]

SWEDENBORG'S THEOLOGY VS. OTHER FORMS OF CHRISTIANITY

Swedenborg presents his theology as essentially Christian, and in fact more truly Christian than either Protestantism or Catholicism, as suggested by the title of his last published work, *True Christianity*. Although he suggests a new direction for Christianity, his theology has much in common with mainstream denominations: He believes in the sacraments of baptism and communion, the latter of which he calls the Holy Supper. He subscribes to the divine inspiration of certain books of Christian Scripture, those he calls the Word (see below). He supports the existence of heaven and hell, angels and devils, and the salvation or condemnation of the individual after death. He urges repentance and the shunning of evils as sins against God. He speaks of faith and goodwill, and recommends performing acts of charity. He believes in the Father, the Son, and the Holy Spirit, and in the divinity of Jesus Christ. Yet in the main both Protestants and Catholics differentiate Swedenborg's theology from their own, as does Swedenborg himself.

His claimed otherworldly experiences give him a radically different perspective on Scripture that occasions much of his departure from mainstream Christianity. He believes that many passages in Scripture are not to be taken literally, and if taken literally are not intelligible or coherent. Take, for example, this passage from *Secrets of Heaven* 3228:

> Anyone can see that material like this does sup-
> ply the religious history of that era but provides
> little for a person's spiritual life—and yet it is our
> spiritual life that the Word exists for. What differ-
> ence does it make knowing who Abraham's sons by
> Keturah were [Genesis 25:2–4], or who Ishmael's
> were [Genesis 25:13–15]? Does it matter that
> Esau became worn out hunting and asked for lentil
> soup, or that Jacob cleverly took the opportunity to
> exchange it for the birthright [Genesis 25:29–34]?[13]

The Word is holy because it has multiple layers of sacred meaning. Its inner spiritual meaning is revealed only to those who read it in a heartfelt search for the truth itself or for knowledge of how they might help themselves and others become more angelic. As will soon be shown, Swedenborg's understanding of certain biblical passages is very different from that of some Roman Catholics and Protestants. Of a great many examples that could be given, two discussed below are the mention of the keys of the kingdom that are given to Peter (Matthew 16:19), and the promised opportunity to rest from labors after death (Revelation 14:13). Although Swedenborg uses many volumes to lay out the inner meaning of Genesis, Exodus, and the Book of Revelation verse by verse,[14] he asserts that there are only three topics in Scripture: the church, heaven, and the Lord (*Sacred Scripture* 16, 17:4). These topics parallel three inner layers of meaning: the internal historical meaning, depicting human spiritual history; the regenerative meaning, portraying the rebirth of the individual; and the supreme meaning, relating Jesus's process of glorification or becoming divine. Scripture is not, he emphasizes, concerned with worldly events. He criticizes those who read the Bible seeking only its literal meaning; the "meaning that shines forth from the Word's literal sense when one examines and unfolds it to confirm some dogma of the church" is more literal than spiritual; the inner meaning is deeper still (*Sacred Scripture* 5).[15]

Upsetting to some mainstream Christians is Swedenborg's creation of a different canon of Scripture through the identification of certain books in the Bible as exclusively constituting the Word because they have a spiritual meaning throughout. At the same time, he holds other books of the Bible to be intermittently spiritual or to lack an inner meaning altogether, and therefore as not constituting the Word, although they are nonetheless "useful books for the church" (*Revelation Explained* [= *Apocalypse Explained*] §815:2).[16] In the same section of *Revelation Explained*, he goes on to say:

> I wish to cite here passages that mention "faith" and "believing," but only passages from the Gospels, not from the Letters of the Apostles. The reason for my doing so is that the Gospels contain the sayings of the Lord himself, all of which have a hidden spiritual meaning, through which direct communication with heaven is possible. There is no comparable meaning within the writings of the Apostles.

Also disturbing to many Christians is Swedenborg's disavowal of three persons in the Godhead. He believes, as mentioned before, in a trinity of aspects, but not of persons, in God. Jesus was the one and only God, born in human form on earth.

Swedenborg presents this view of God as the central tenet of the New Church. His disavowal of a trinity of persons leads to a reframing of many other Christian concepts: Redemption was not achieved through a sacrifice on the cross, but through a restoration of spiritual freedom as the result of a reorganization of the heavens and the hells. Christ's merit is not something we can borrow like a cloak at the hour of our death, but a power we can call on as we expend effort to improve ourselves spiritually. The Lord saves all who have indicated by the way they live that they truly desire to be saved, but he will not intercede in any extraordinary way for those who have chosen to be evil at heart, even if they have been baptized and profess to have faith in him.

Any concept that implies an angry God and Jesus's sacrifice to appease him Swedenborg rejects out of hand. God was not angry, nor did the Son come into the world to satisfy the Father's rage. The Father did not look at the Son bleeding on the Cross and change his mind about condemning the human race. The Son does not now literally sit at the right hand of a separately existing God the Father and send out a separately existing Holy Spirit. Swedenborg portrays these concepts of God as ludicrous and damaging; none of them would be consonant with pure love and mercy.

Swedenborg rejects the vicarship of the pope and the intercession of Mary and the saints. The Lord alone has divine authority and leads the church; he alone is the gate to the fold of heaven. Peter, to whom Jesus gave the keys, means not the disciple himself but the faith in the Lord he symbolically represents. Swedenborg also rejects monastic approaches to spiritual life, insisting that the only way to a full, useful, and joyful life in heaven is through a full, useful, and joyful life in this world, including its politics, business, and social and family life.

Swedenborg rejects the doctrine of original sin. Adam and Eve's actions did not curse the human race. (The biblical Adam and Eve were not individuals but figures standing for the people of the earliest church.) Swedenborg's theology includes only two types of evil: hereditary and actual. Hereditary evil takes the form of inclinations or tendencies toward evil passed from one generation to the next. Actual evil refers to the evil acts we commit. Hereditary evil is not at all damning, because it cannot be helped. Actual evil becomes sinful and damning only if we do it knowingly and deliberately and we never repent.

Although some branches of Christianity have many sacraments, Swedenborg recognizes but two: baptism and the Holy Supper.[17] Their point and efficacy are spiritual and symbolic rather than physical. Swedenborg characterizes these two sacraments as gates at either end of a large field. We go through the gate of baptism to enter the church, and through the gate of the Holy Supper to enter heaven while still on earth (*True Christianity* 721). Although Swedenborg does mention the need for worship and ritual observance, his works present it as a secondary aspect of religious life; primary is the individual's repentance and useful service to others.

Baptism is appropriate not only for infants but for adults as well. It does not grant or guarantee salvation, but it attests that participants are part of the church. The water and the sign of the cross symbolize being cleansed and saved by learning truth about the Lord and undergoing spiritual crises. The Holy Supper affords partnership with heaven to those who approach in the right frame of heart and mind. And even if the heart and mind are not in the right place, the Holy Supper still affords the Lord's presence. Both the bread and the wine are to be taken, as they symbolize the love for the Lord and the faith in the Lord necessary for salvation.

There is no condemnation, Swedenborg teaches, of children who die, whether baptized or not (*Heaven and Hell* 329–45). All people who die before reaching adulthood go to heaven, although he does not specify a minimum age of death by which people have made a choice of heaven or hell. Although all human beings have hereditary inclinations toward evil, children who die have not yet had a chance to commit purposeful, adult, actual evil, and so nothing impedes their salvation. They have free choice, but all freely choose to go to heaven. At one point Swedenborg writes that infants make up "a third part of heaven" (*Heaven and Hell* 4). Given the number of young children who die, it would make sense to interpret this phrase as "one third of heaven" rather than as "a third distinct heaven," but the Latin is as ambiguous as its English translation.

Swedenborg dismisses the notion of a single Devil who started out as an angel of light and then fell, taking a crew of others with him. Swedenborg uses the terms *the Devil* and *Satan* instead to denote hell in the aggregate. He also uses the plural to denote inhabitants of different parts of hell, devils being those who love evil, and satans those who think and believe falsely (*Heaven and Hell* 311, 544).

The notion of predestination to hell Swedenborg greets with a special expression of horror and distaste, calling it "insane" (*True Christianity* 56, 487:5), "cruel" (*Divine Providence* 330:8; *True Christianity* 486:3, 487:5), and "hurtful" (*Survey* 66:3;

True Christianity 486:3). The only true form of predestination, he says, is God's intention that everyone should go to heaven, although the individual is free to thwart that intention. False is the notion that the chosen few or the elect have foreordained places in heaven, while the rest of humanity is simply condemned without recourse, as it goes against the concept of a God who is pure love and mercy (*Survey* 66).

Although Swedenborg agrees with the Christian notion that there is no time and space in heaven, he adds a qualification: there is an *appearance* of space and time in the spiritual world, and that appearance is real because it is fixed and constant, anchored not to physical motion but to the states of mind of those who live there (*True Christianity* 29). To the apocryphal quibble about how many angels can dance on the head of a pin, Swedenborg might reply that the same number of angels could dance on the head of a spiritual pin as physical bodies could dance on a physical pin—that is, none.

Swedenborg says that the eternal "rest from labors" promised in Revelation 14:13 does not mean that angels are perpetually idle. In fact he maintains quite the opposite. "Labors" in that passage refers not to useful activity but to the spiritual effort in "being tested"—effort that comes to an end as we become ready for heaven (*Revelation Unveiled* 640). Idleness is no blessing; the very joy of heaven comes from useful activity. All angels have jobs, positions, and functions. Angels' marriages are nourished and made more delightful by their useful activity. The life of heaven as Swedenborg portrays it is a full and concrete life. Unlike traditional Christian images of genderless angels endlessly playing harps in praise of God, Swedenborg's angels are female and male; they have stimulating marriages and jobs; they have homes, streets, and gardens, and lives more useful and varied than our own.[18]

SWEDENBORG'S THEOLOGY VS.
OTHER MODERN RELIGIOUS PERSPECTIVES

Swedenborg's views variously embrace and challenge not only mainstream Christianity, but other modern religious perspectives as well. Wouter Hanegraaff has pointed out Swedenborg's "highly significant and widely influential" contribution to the amorphous spiritual movement commonly known as the New Age.[19] There is much for the New Age and other modern religious perspectives to love in Swedenborg's theology: the existence of spirits and the possibility (however dangerous) of human interaction with them; the notion of correspondence between the spiritual world and the physical world; the focus on the human anatomy, including the notion of body memory (the storing of life events in physical parts of the body); the idea of inflow; Swedenborg's use of gardens for connection with the spiritual world; and his recognition of the energy or auras around rocks and plants and human beings.[20]

Many of Swedenborg's views, however, distance him from the New Age. For example, his system leaves no room for reincarnation. The individual remains the individual after death. We have one life that begins when we are born, and never ends. Our body breathes and lives, and eventually dies; our spirit then awakens in the spiritual world, undergoes a process of teaching and self-evaluation that ultimately results in reduction to our own inner essence, and finally finds a home in heaven or hell, where it remains to all eternity. Swedenborg makes no mention of people shifting from one heaven to another, or transferring in any permanent way from hell to heaven, or coming back to earth, or being aware of the details of their upcoming lives on earth. In fact, he calls the idea that the soul of one person could pass into another an "absurd notion" (*True Christianity* 171) and implies rejection of other such beliefs in *True Christianity* 79:6 and *Heaven and Hell* 183. Swedenborg writes that the notion of reincarnation resulted from occasional leaks from spirits' memories into human memories, making people think they had had previous lives. He adds, however, that this phenomenon is rare, and that the usual order of things is that the spirits who are with us experience our memory as their own (*Heaven and Hell* 256, 298).

Swedenborg's view of hell may endear him to few modern readers. Seen in heaven's light, hell is a miserable, polluted place, largely barren of vegetation, in constant political turmoil, where excruciating pain is the only remaining form of social control and restraint. The newcomer's first few hours are pleasant enough, while he or she is being sized up by those already there. After that, life consists in enslaving and being enslaved, working for food and shelter in cavernous workhouses, and indulging in lust and avarice after hours, while the agony of deserved punishment gradually reduces the desire to attack the Lord and angels to a smoldering coal, never quite extinguished and certainly never replaced by goodness. There is no parole. Hell itself is eternal, and so is the individual's stay in it.[21]

Nevertheless, even in his description of hell Swedenborg conveys the Lord's love. To dwell in hell is the individual's choice, freely made. The Lord could not and would not take that away, or transplant someone to a heaven they would find repellent and even physically intolerable. Hell is governed entirely by the Lord and is magnificently arranged and sorted in three dimensions according to varieties of evil. There is no literal fire or gnashing of teeth. Heaven's light only occasionally intrudes and shows the reality of their situation; most of the time they are spared. In their own light, the devils look human to each other and their world looks normal and even pleasing. They are allowed to indulge their evil fantasies and sexual desires as long as they do not hurt others beyond what those others deserve. The Lord's love for the inhabitants of hell allows them a godless, unreal world whose only major frustration, but a significant one, is the limit set on their cruelty and revenge.

Another teaching that may rankle some modern readers is that human beings go to heaven and have eternal life, but animals do not. Animals do not have a human soul, and only the human soul lives forever. A human being is not merely an ape with extraordinary language skills and social problems. Animals are born already knowing everything they need to know. Human infants know almost nothing, not even enough to prevent them from putting harmful objects in their mouths (*Marriage Love* 133). What humans have that animals lack is the quality of being completely empty at birth, which allows them to be filled without end. An animal, which will never be much more than it was at birth, is unable to depart from the order of its life. People can and do depart from the order of their lives, but this risk is compensated for by the fact that they can also achieve eternal bliss and endless growth in heaven. Therefore, Swedenborg says, animals' perfection at birth becomes their imperfection, while humans' imperfection at birth becomes their perfection (*True Christianity* 48:9).

Swedenborg explains that there are plants and animals on earth that were not originally part of creation (*Divine Love and Wisdom* 339). Corresponding to human evil loves and false thoughts, predatory animals and toxic plants came into being after creation as the human race fell. Still, their harmfulness and savagery is confined, he writes, to the need to protect and nourish themselves. Human savagery is much worse. Swedenborg holds that humane qualities, although acquirable in the course of life through religion and spirituality, are not native to the human race.

Swedenborg's attitude to nature, like that of his contemporaries, is also out of step with some modern views. Although he sees heavenly wonders in bees and silkworms, when it comes to vegetation his writings, like his property, treasure cultivation. Heaven is not like a wilderness but like a garden. Hell is sand and rock or, at most, nature gone to seed: "Where there is any vegetation, brambles, stinging nettles, thorns, thistles, and certain poisonous plants spring up. Alternately, the vegetation disappears and you see only stones in piles and swamps where frogs croak" (*True Christianity* 78:5).

Repentance of the mind parallels tilling of the soil.

> Before repentance we are like a wilderness where there are terrifying wild beasts, dragons, screech owls, vipers, and snakes whose bite causes unstoppable bleeding, and in the thickets there are howling birds of night, and there satyrs dance. But when these creatures have been cast out by our work and

effort, that wilderness can be plowed and made ready for planting, and sown first with oats, beans, and flax, and afterward with barley and wheat.[22]

Nature is not heavenly when left to itself but becomes heavenly through work and cultivation. This attitude on Swedenborg's part is evident even in the decorative ornaments in his first editions, which feature gardening and cultivation.[23]

FOUR

Problematic Content

Swedenborg's theological garden contains views that, like the taste of unfamiliar fruit, some readers might find offensive or incredible, whatever their background. In addition to the theological departures outlined above, three controversial areas concern his statements about women, about Jews, and about human beings on other planets.

Some have seen a bias against women in Swedenborg's writings. *Marriage Love,* for example, seems to lay out a double standard in which virginity is a vital attribute of brides (*Marriage Love* 503, 504:2), but a merely preferable attribute of bridegrooms, expected of only "a few" (*Marriage Love* 459:1, 460:5).[1] In the main, though, Swedenborg's treatment of men and women is remarkably balanced, particularly if one takes into account the largely male readership of the time. He is an adamant proponent of monogamy and of equality in marriage. He asserts that domination by either the husband or the wife completely destroys the love in a marriage (*Heaven and Hell* 380). Women are capable of domination—they are, if anything, a stronger rather than a weaker sex; by nature they possess the power and skill to subject their husbands to "the yoke of their authority" if they wish (*Marriage Love* 292). They also possess an extrasensory perception unknown to men (*Marriage Love* 155b:4).

One central teaching, however, favors fathers genetically over mothers. Swedenborg maintains that our soul comes from our father alone (*True Christianity* 103). Our mother contributes our body and our lower mind, but our soul and inner life is exclusively from our father.[2] Unlike other challenging but merely illustrative statements Swedenborg makes,[3] this concept is integral to the heart of his theology. Jesus was divine, because his Father was divine; Jesus's soul was the life itself that created the universe. All that Jesus inherited from Mary were the lower aspects of human nature that he put off in the process of glorification, including the flesh and hereditary inclinations to every form of evil. Although that process was indescribably intense and took over three decades, success was possible because Jesus inherited his soul and life exclusively from his "father," meaning God himself. This, explains Swedenborg, is why Jesus never acknowledged Mary as his mother, and why Mary, speaking to Swedenborg once in the spiritual world, said that although she gave birth to Jesus, ever since he became fully divine she has not wanted people to view him as her son (*True Christianity* 102).

As for Jews, Swedenborg writes more than a dozen hard statements about those of Old Testament times, saying that they utterly lacked interest in things spiritual and as a result were idolatrous, cruel, contemptuous, vengeful, and unforgiving.[4] The Jews of his own day he also criticizes over a dozen times, characterizing them as adulterous, avaricious, and still closed to spiritual truth.[5] Nevertheless he mentions exceptions: "better" Jews, Jews who are open to spiritual instruction in the other world, and Jews who live in mutual love without contempt;[6] and he says that when Jews are mentioned in Scripture they have the highest of connotations: they mean all who live in the goodness of love

(*Divine Providence* 260; *Revelation Unveiled* 96, 182). Given the Holocaust, which occurred long after Swedenborg's lifetime, it is important to note that there is in his works no advocacy of violence against Jews or will for their destruction. On the contrary, his remarks concerning them are immovably embedded in a clear context of love and respect for all humankind (*True Christianity* 406–7), which accords with his own practice in life.

Comments of this kind were common in a place and time marked by prolonged, intense religious warfare; they were made in a spirit of zeal for what the observers saw as the truth. But unlike the anti-Jewish remarks of many of his contemporaries, Swedenborg's comments are clearly not part of a prejudice in favor of contemporary Christianity, the learned, the clergy, and Western Europe. That is, he does not single Jews out for notice. He makes sweeping, often negative, characterizations of other world religions, especially Catholicism, and of various European nationalities. He often asserts that the learned compare poorly with the simple, the clergy compare poorly with the laity, Christians compare poorly with non-Christians, Europeans compare poorly with Africans and the Chinese, and the inhabitants of Earth compare poorly with the inhabitants of other planets.

Life on other planets is the third area that some might find problematic. Swedenborg maintains that there is life on every planetlike body, including the moon that orbits our earth. He asserts that to believe anything else would be to underestimate the divine love. Given the Lord's primary goal of a heaven from the human race, why else, he argues, would planets exist except to support human beings and ultimately populate heaven?[7] He reports his conversations with spirits from other planets, and passes on from them sociological and political information about

life on their planets. In his work *Other Planets* he reports inter-
actions with spirits from Mercury, Venus, Mars, Jupiter, Saturn,
and our moon, as well as five other planets from outside our solar
system. In all of his discussion of other planets, Swedenborg's
central point is clear: he aims to show that the worship of the
Lord is not simply an Earth-centered religion. Jesus Christ is
God of the entire universe. God chose to be born on this earth
because, unlike other planets, the Earth has sustained written
languages and global commerce for thousands of years. God was
also born here because this earth is spiritually the lowest and
outermost planet, and by coming from the highest to the lowest
point he would bridge all points in between (see *Other Planets*
122).[8]

FIVE

Unusual Specimens and the Doorway to the Mirror Garden

any readers have noted the large-scale features of Swedenborg's theological garden just summarized. These features are hard to miss because Swedenborg frequently repeats his main points. However, like the specimens of exotic flora, the strange and wonderful little buildings, and the maze in Swedenborg's garden, his published theological works incorporate many striking and noteworthy small-scale features that have rarely received notice.

The Unique and Intriguing

When strolling through Swedenborg's individual sections, one frequently comes upon unusual concepts of few words but extensive implications, like a single imported flower in Swedenborg's garden that stands for an otherwise unrepresented continent. For example, just once Swedenborg mentions gorgeous temples on another planet woven and pruned into shape out of whole groves of still-living trees, with prisms between the leaves splashing colored sunlight inside (*Other Planets* 151).

Elsewhere, in a discussion of the four directions in heaven, Swedenborg briefly mentions spiritual gravity (*Heaven and Hell* 142). He points out that gravity gives all who live on earth a common center, to which the lowest parts of their bodies are closest. Heaven, he says, has a spiritual gravity that affects all its inhabitants, but the front of the body and the face are closest to the common center there, the Lord. In three and a half million words, this intriguing concept of spiritual gravity occurs but once.

Likewise at the end of a chapter on heavenly language that maintains there is one universal language in heaven, Swedenborg appends a brief but provocative list of other heavenly languages, including languages of facial expressions, images, bodily movements, shared feelings and thoughts, and perhaps most intriguingly, thunder (*Heaven and Hell* 244).

In another part of Swedenborg's theological garden one comes upon a single mention of atmospheric and rainbow heavens:

> There is a heaven containing atmospheres of various colors, in which the whole air flashes as if with gold, silver, pearls, precious stones, flowers in tiny forms, and countless other substances. There is also a rainbow heaven, containing the most beautiful rainbows, great and small, varied with the most vivid colors.[1]

Although Swedenborg wrote this early in his theological period and later produced an entire work on heaven, he never mentions these particular heavens again.`

A strange and fascinating structure in the garden of Swedenborg's theology is his involvement in the affairs of the spiritual world, as portrayed in his accounts of memorable occurrences (narratives of his experiences in the spiritual realm).[2] He does not draw attention in his writings to the role he plays in the other world, or its contrast with his role in this world; yet phrases now and then depict him as a preacher and teacher in the spiritual world, widely traveled, famous to some, notorious to others, having extraordinary powers and protection from evil. Swedenborg travels to all levels of heaven, including areas for spirits from other planets; to all areas of the world of spirits, including its region closest to hell, known as the lower earth; and to areas of hell. He teaches angels (*True Christianity* 76; *Marriage Love* 444). Spirits identify him as one who has been preaching repentance in the other world, whose message is so unwelcome to the evil that when he fell sick and lay apparently dead they felt joy and relief (*Revelation Unveiled* 531). He stretches out his hands and as a result evil creatures attack people who are threatening him (*Marriage Love* 79:10). He is asked to do miracles and tell the future, and refuses not because he is unable but because it would not induce belief (*Marriage Love* 535). He interacts with devils without being harmed, even using them to conduct spiritual experiments (*Marriage Love* 444:6–7). He repeatedly expresses surprise at the level of protection from malicious spirits granted him by the Lord (*Secrets of Heaven* 59:2, 699, 5863, 7479), and even derives benefit from his interaction with such spirits (*Secrets of Heaven* 968, 7479).

HUMOR IN SWEDENBORG

Here and there, in an orchard of Swedenborgian seriousness, one encounters slender shoots of subtle humor. At times it occurs in similes. For example, Swedenborg writes that the effort to link genuine kindness and goodwill to a belief in three gods is "like a carriage with horses that are attached to it only by the reins in the driver's hands; when the horses start to run they pull the driver from his seat, leaving the carriage behind" (*True Christianity* 451). Another passage similarly verging on slapstick warns that we should not affirm things in Scripture that are not genuinely true. To do so would cause heaven to turn from us, just as a person would turn away if spattered by a bursting balloon full of gall (*True Christianity* 258). In one passage Swedenborg sees a group of spirits whose manner of speech is like "a heap of filthy garbage overflowing its container. The intellectual element of it was presented as the backside of a horse whose forequarters could not be seen" (*Secrets of Heaven* 1644:2).

Shoots of humor occur especially in the areas of the textual garden called accounts of memorable occurrences. He reports having so challenged a spirit on his belief in faith alone that the spirit picked up a lighted candlestick to throw at him. The flame went out, however, and in the ensuing darkness the spirit hit his companion in the forehead instead, and Swedenborg laughed (*Revelation Unveiled* 484:6). During a discussion of promiscuity at another point, Swedenborg conjectures to satyrlike spirits that Circe, the sorceress of Greek myth, must have turned the wandering hero Ulysses' men not into pigs, as the legend holds, but into adulterers. The satyr-spirits find this idea and other jests of Swedenborg's raucously amusing (*Marriage Love* 521:4).

It is hard not to see humor in Swedenborg's depiction of people who think heaven will consist of eternally glorifying God. On day two of a three-day locked-in-church compulsory worship service, an angel suggests that Swedenborg "see how they are glorifying God." Swedenborg discovers that most are sleeping, and the rest are either yawning or wild-eyed, oppressed at heart and weary in spirit. They finally overcome their guards, break open the doors that confine them, and escape (*Marriage Love* 9:2).

Similarly, the people who think heaven consists of spending all eternity in paradisal gardens enjoying bucolic delights find a hellish monotony when these desires materialize. After three days of quaffing freshly squeezed juices, weaving garlands, singing melodies, and playing with water fountains, their ennui is so great that a number wander in circles begging for the way out, only to be told by some prankster that they are in the very middle of heaven, in the center of its delights, where they may stay forever (*Marriage Love* 8:1–3).

Some of the humor in Swedenborg's Latin is difficult to translate. For instance, in a speech to other national groups English spirits attribute sexual potency to physical strength and good health. At the end they follow a complex sentence 109 words long with a one-word pun, "*Vale*," which means both "goodbye" and "be strong."[3]

ASYMMETRIES IN THE GARDEN

From time to time in Swedenborg's published theological works one finds something especially significant that appears to be out of place, like the sunflowers he planted among the many types of roses in the rose garden.[4] For example, Swedenborg devotes a small volume to the topic of Scripture, yet in it he does not tackle the subject of the canon of Scripture or define "the Word" other than to say it is divine truth (*Sacred Scripture* 1). To find the list of books of the Bible that he considers to be the Word, one needs to read instead the work on Genesis and Exodus or the survey of teachings of the New Jerusalem.[5] Likewise, Swedenborg's book

with hell in the title, *Heaven and Hell,* includes no mention of
cavernous workhouses there; yet in a work expounding the Book
of Revelation, Swedenborg describes cavernous workhouses in
detail and asserts that all of hell consists of nothing but such
workhouses (*Revelation Unveiled* 153).

Then there are elements that remind the reader of the mir-
rored "doorway" off to one side of his garden in Stockholm
that reflected the scene behind the viewer; it allowed people to
glimpse the illusion of another full garden. Swedenborg told
people that he found the reflected garden much more beautiful
than the real one.[6] Likewise, there are elements in Swedenborg's
theology mentioned in pairs, but rather than discussing both
aspects equally, Swedenborg emphasizes one over the other. Bal-
ancing, as he often does, the designations "heavenly" (or celestial)
and "spiritual," Swedenborg points to the existence of a complete
layer of meaning running throughout Scripture called the heavenly meaning, and another complete layer called the spiritual
meaning. They are equally extensive, so to speak, although the
heavenly meaning is higher and more profound than the spiritual. Yet the heavenly meaning takes up far less space in Swedenborg's texts. He devotes over five thousand quarto pages to
unfolding the spiritual meaning, while the heavenly meaning he
acknowledges but briefly a few times, rarely articulating what
it is.[7] Only once does he justify this seeming imbalance, stating
that the heavenly meaning is difficult to explain "because it does
not relate to the thoughts of our intellect as much as to the emotions of our will" (*Sacred Scripture* 19). The heavenly meaning is
a vast area reflected in a small, mysterious mirror.[8]

Swedenborg repeatedly indicates that there is a great deal he
cannot say.[9] He finds it impossible to convey some aspects of his

spiritual experiences. The limitations of human language and the transcendent nature of heavenly experience thwart his efforts at verbalization.

Swedenborg also omits material for reasons other than inexpressibility, presumably (although he does not say so directly) to leave room for the reader's participation. For example, his explanations of the inner meaning of the Word seem more like a rudimentary algebra by which the reader might eventually solve an equation than like the solution itself. Take his treatment of the following passage in Matthew:

> The lamp of the body is the eye. If your eye is simple, your whole body will be full of light; but if your eye is evil, your whole body will be full of darkness. If then the light that is in you is darkness, how great a darkness! (Matthew 6:22–23)

At five points in his published theological works Swedenborg discusses this passage. In four of them, he gives the inner meaning of the eye and of no other element (*Secrets of Heaven* 2701:2, 2973:5, 9548:7; *Revelation Unveiled* 48); in the fifth he also explains one other element, the darkness (*Secrets of Heaven* 9051:2). He could have explained much more, however, as he does in four *unpublished* explanations of the same verses.[10] Swedenborg's incomplete exposition in the published works seems less like the garden itself than like a doorway to an otherwise invisible garden.

Another asymmetry in the garden of Swedenborg's theology concerns its practicality. Swedenborg categorically opposes faith alone and emphasizes that to bring salvation, belief has to be accompanied by action. "All religion has to do with life, and the life of religion is to do good" (*Life* 1). Without the work of repentance, and actions of love, goodwill, and useful service, we cannot reach heaven. Yet although he emphasizes life, in many areas there is little specific instruction on how to live. More than 150 times, for example, Swedenborg mentions meditating or meditation. Many of the accounts of memorable occurrences begin with a reference to Swedenborg meditating.[11] Yet Swedenborg does not define or describe what meditation is, nor does he offer advice on how to go about it. Likewise he gives the inner meaning of countless passages in Scripture, and strongly encourages readers to explore Scripture for themselves, but does not give thorough expositions nor lay out a detailed methodology for finding the inner meaning.[12]

In the area of repentance, though, he does give practical advice. A whole chapter in *True Christianity* gives an organized presentation with steps to follow and illustrative examples. It may be that the practical advice lacking in other areas is offered in this one because the individual needs to go through repentance to establish a partnership with the Lord. Once that partnership is forged, the Lord will lead the individual and supply things that Swedenborg's text cannot provide, as the following strikingly direct passage suggests:

> My friend, abstain from what is evil, do what is good, and believe in the Lord with your whole heart and your whole soul, and the Lord will love you, and give you love with which to act and faith with which to believe. Then with love you will do

what is good, and with trust and confidence you will believe; and if you persevere, you will come into the reciprocal and perpetual partnership [with the Lord] that is salvation itself and eternal life. (*True Christianity* 484)

The Style of Swedenborg's
Published Theological Works

The style of Swedenborg's works is similar to their content, and both resemble the garden on the grounds where they were written. In the main, Swedenborg's theological prose style is simple and unadorned; yet small-scale features exhibit a variety of dramatic and poetical colors: descriptive accounts of extraordinary experiences, dialogs in a variety of voices, poetic diction, similes, and subtle allusions to many disciplines and areas of life. The transitions into poeticisms are often abrupt, as Swedenborg rarely forges explicit connections between them and the cognitive flow of the text. A chapter soberly explaining the inner meaning of Revelation 9 is immediately followed by the recounting of a spiritual experience in which children give expensive gifts to two-headed tortoises who rise out of the ocean to lick the children's hands (*Revelation Unveiled* 463).

In his theological works Swedenborg incorporated more and more poetical features as he went along. The first work (*Secrets of Heaven*) has few; the last work (*True Christianity*), many. The overall effect is that of a coherent, interesting talk increasingly punctuated by a silent showing of seemingly unrelated yet colorful visuals. As the presence of such dramatic and poetical features in a theological text seems unusual, a brief account of the history of Swedenborg's Latin styles may be useful.

NEO-LATIN AND SWEDENBORG'S EARLIER WRITINGS

Swedenborg engaged in writing and publishing over his entire lifetime, from age twelve to age eighty-three. Before his spiritual crisis he wrote volumes in one of two distinct styles: the explanatory or the poetical. (These terms are discussed more fully below.) Although a work in the explanatory style might include an occasional poetical passage,[1] or a work in the poetical style might include footnotes in the explanatory style (*Worship and Love of God*), a given volume was generally in one style or the other, not both. In his theological volumes, however, we find both of these styles within the same binding, although they remain distinct. By the time of his last publication (*True Christianity*) the poetical style had become as prominent as the explanatory.

Swedenborg used the Neo-Latin language as the vehicle for the eighteen theological works he published between 1749 and 1771. There have been three great ages of literary Latin: classical Latin, medieval Latin, and Neo-Latin. Throughout the history of Latin there was also a spoken language of the common people, which has been difficult to reach through written texts.[2] Classical Latin as it has been handed down is a relatively artificial language of writing and oratory that developed alongside ancient Roman culture. Medieval Latin was born in the hands of the first Latin translators of the Greek New Testament, people of the lower classes who cast the New Testament in a simpler Latin, presumably something like the spoken language. Medieval Latin was later spoken in churches and in the classrooms of the early universities. From the Renaissance onward, as classical Latin was rediscovered and rewoven with the spoken Medieval Latin of church and classroom, and as scientific developments forced the creation of new Latin vocabulary, Neo-Latin came into being.

When Swedenborg first encountered Neo-Latin in the late seventeenth century, it was enjoying its golden age in Sweden (1680–1720). Swedenborg grew up hearing professors lecture, orators declaim, and poets hold forth at the University of Uppsala in a high form of the dialect.[3]

By his mid-twenties Swedenborg had mastered the art of Neo-Latin poetry sufficiently to publish a volume of his own poems that came out in two editions, and two highly poetical prose works full of mythological and literary allusions to Greek and Latin classics.[4]

Later, in his thirties, forties, and fifties, as he turned to writing on mineralogy, philosophy, and anatomy, Swedenborg cultivated a straightforward and humble, almost conversational, explanatory style, with a large but accessible vocabulary. In the preface to his 1734 work *The Infinite* he gives his reasons:

> Here you see Philosophy reasoning about the Infinite and the soul, using perfectly familiar words and a humble style; that is, without terms hunted up from her metaphysical stockroom. This is to prevent anything unfamiliar or elevated in the words from holding the mind back or distracting it by making it ponder on the terms themselves. In discussing an elevated topic, one must make every effort to avoid the least word that might pose an obstacle. For this

reason I wanted Philosophy to present herself as
simply as possible, in the terms people use when
speaking with friends.[5]

In 1745, not long after his spiritual experiences began, he set
this simple style aside to philosophize in complex and poetical
prose in *Worship and Love of God,* a work that was partly published but never completed even in draft. After devoting the
next four years to biblical research, he began publishing his set
of eighteen theological titles. Although *Worship and Love of God*
addresses theological topics, Swedenborg himself does not present it as one of his theological works, and none of the other
eighteen titles (which are heavily cross-referenced) refers back to
it. *Worship and Love of God* stands alone as a unique transitional
work, written shortly after Swedenborg's spiritual awakening,
and showing both the scientific and the philosophical interests
that had dominated the previous decades, as well as presaging
the theological interests that would dominate his writing in the
decades to come.[6]

Swedenborg's Theological Latin Styles

For his theological works Swedenborg crafted a Latin style that
was even simpler than the explanatory scientific Latin he had
used before. Latin readers both in his day and in ours have noted
the remarkable simplicity and straightforwardness of his theological writing.[7] His style was extraordinarily simple compared
with that of his contemporaries.[8] Yet Swedenborg was one of
the best-educated people in Europe at the time. Elements of
both the style and the content of his published theological works
reflect his panoramic interests: biblical and ecclesiastical studies,

liturgy and rubric, as well as study of world religions contemporary and ancient; philosophy; geometry, calculus, and other forms of mathematics; anatomy, astronomy, botany, chemistry, metallurgy, and other sciences; classical literature and mythology, oratory, poetry, narrative, simile, dialog, drama, music, art, and sculpture; sports; education, history, geography, agriculture, economics, politics, law, business, trade, and travel; and the domestic world of marriage, home, and family. Like his garden, then, Swedenborg's theological Neo-Latin shows an overarching order and simplicity, while specific features exhibit a variety and diversity that verge on the global.

As we approach Swedenborg's theological Neo-Latin more closely we first see the two distinct Latin styles of prose mentioned above: an explanatory style and a poetical one. By the ancient table of *genera dicendi* (types of speaking) established by classical orators, the *explanatory style* would be a low or simple style, designed to inform.[9] Most of its nouns come from a short list of heavily repeated abstract words that are linked to and defined by each other. The following example is quite typical:

> Since the truth of our perceptions depends on our intent for good, "servants" means people who are intent on seeing things truly because they want to do good. It also means people who are filled with wisdom because they are moved by love, since wisdom is concerned with what is true and love is concerned with what is good. It also means people who see things in the light of their faith because they care, since faith too is concerned with what is true and caring is concerned with what is good.[10]

Most of the verbs in the explanatory style are forms of the verb *to be* or abstract verbs in the passive voice, generally in the present tense. The clauses are logically subordinated and heavily nested,[11] and the sentences often follow a deductive path from a premise to a conclusion.

Swedenborg's explanatory style during the theological period is the simplest he ever wrote. Latinist Alvar Erikson has documented some of the changes in Swedenborg's syntax and vocabulary that attended his shift toward an even simpler and more conversational prose. Most notably, Swedenborg uses a nonclassical construction for expressing what grammarians call indirect discourse.[12] His explanatory Latin follows a simple, rather Germanic, word order rather than the convoluted word order of classical literary Latin. It does not stray, however, into Latin that is colloquial or incorrect, avoiding the many barbarous Latin forms then in circulation. His explanatory style is quite straightforward and unadorned.

The *poetical style* is markedly different. Although Swedenborg always uses prose to express his theology, and much of it is written in an explanatory style that is wholly prosaic, at times he uses a poetical style of prose corresponding to the middle style of the *genera dicendi,* designed to engage the imagination. The poetical style employs a large vocabulary of concrete nouns. Its verbs, too, are concrete; they are usually active in voice, in either past or present tense, and their clauses are linked side by side with coordinate conjunctions. The following example is a simile in *True Christianity.*

> They could also be compared to people who weave
> a life raft out of rushes and reeds, using tar to glue it

together; and they set out onto the great expanse of
the ocean, but out there the tar glue dissolves; and
suffocated by the briny water, they are swallowed up
and buried in its depths. (*True Christianity* 342:3)

For much of Swedenborg's theological period the poetical style
rarely occurs, but it increases dramatically in frequency toward
the end.

The most voluminous form that the poetical style takes
toward the end of Swedenborg's theological period is the cat-
egory of text that Swedenborg labels *memorabilia*—the accounts
of memorable occurrences, traditionally known as memorable
relations, which have already been mentioned above. These
lengthy narratives of specific spiritual experiences recounted in
the past tense often include extensive dialog with spirits and
angels. There is a great variety among the voices that Swedenborg quotes: some sound simple; others hold forth in the highest
form of elocution anywhere in Swedenborg's published theology (*Marriage Love* 111). In accounts of memorable occurrences
Swedenborg will even at times depart from standard prose
vocabulary to use a pointedly poetical diction.[13]

In Swedenborg's first editions, an account of a memorable
occurrence or a set of memorable occurrences is usually typo-
graphically separated from the main text by large asterisks.[14] At
the beginning of each account Swedenborg labels it a *memorabile*
in small capitals and, where there is more than one, gives an ordi-
nal designation also in small capitals: THE FIFTH MEMORABLE
OCCURRENCE. There is rarely any explicit connection with the
preceding text or with other accounts of memorable occurrences
when they occur together.

When an account of a memorable occurrence first appears (marked out as such) at the end of *Divine Providence* (1764), the thirteenth of the eighteen titles, Swedenborg asks the reader's forgiveness for including it to fill up the rest of the page.[15] From then on, however, they appear in every work. In his next work, *Revelation Unveiled* (1766), accounts of memorable occurrences appear at the end of every chapter. In two cover letters that Swedenborg sent out with *Revelation Unveiled* he draws the addressees' attention to these accounts, and suggests that they be read first.[16] Swedenborg also arranged for a handbill in England promoting *Revelation Unveiled* that advertised its accounts of memorable occurrences, giving the section reference for each one.[17] Accounts of memorable occurrences are even more prominent in the next work in sequence, *Marriage Love* (1768). It begins with over twenty quarto pages of them, and has on average two memorable occurrences after each brief chapter. Some accounts of memorable occurrences appear in *Soul-Body Interaction* (1769) and in *Survey* (1769); and many grace the last work of the set, *True Christianity* (1771).

Another poetical form, the complex simile, blossoms even later than the accounts of memorable occurrences. Swedenborg uses similes with a formulaic introduction to compare theological abstractions to earthly realities, although he often includes intriguing, apparently superfluous, details.[18] Like accounts of memorable occurrences, similes at times display poetical diction;[19] unlike accounts of memorable occurrences, they are not set apart from the main text but occur within it. Although complex similes crop up sporadically in earlier works (see, for example, *Sacred Scripture* 33 and *Divine Providence* 199:2, 211:2), they occur in unique and sudden abundance in *True Christianity*, Swedenborg's last major published theological work. Swedenborg incorporates over four hundred of them into this book,[20] often using two or three, and in one extreme passage (*True Christianity* 348) fourteen of them in a row, to illustrate a single teaching. Although the simple explanatory style predominates in the other seventeen titles, and although *True Christianity's* explanatory articulation is so strong that Swedenborg uses the work's table of contents as an example of truths that come together to form structures that are like fascicles of nerves (§351:1), nevertheless the lengthy accounts of memorable occurrences after chapters and the abundant complex similes and other forms of imagery within chapters make *True Christianity* word for word about half explanatory, half poetical.[21]

The Labyrinthine Maze
of Swedenborg's Theological Style

In Swedenborg's garden there was also a labyrinthine maze.[22] Mirroring Swedenborg's physical garden, when tracing Swedenborg's thoughts through his sentences, we find ourselves at times in a mental labyrinth. Swedenborg even suggests that he crafted the Latin style used in his theological works for protection of the truth.

The reason behind this is evidently that all things sacred are carefully protected. For example, Swedenborg writes that access to the heaven of the earliest people is heavily guarded. Once, struck with an ardent desire to see it, he journeyed there with an angel guide through a dark forest full of intersecting and misleading pathways (*Marriage Love* 75). Responding to their prayers and approving the usefulness of their mission, the Lord granted Swedenborg and his guide the ability to see the occasional olive trees laden with grape vines that marked the true course through the maze.

Likewise, Swedenborg asserts, the treasures in the heart of the Word are not open to the approach of all. A heart and mind turned toward the Lord are necessary for finding our way through the many statements and implications, the many layers of meaning. Although at its center the Word contains a Garden of Eden with food and living water, those who have not found the right viewing angle see only a forest, and those who come from the wrong angle see sand without even grass growing on it (*Sacred Scripture* 96).

In his own writings Swedenborg may have sought to produce something as labyrinthine and self-protecting as the Word and the earliest heaven. A rough note to himself written less than two years before his death suggests that he crafted his prose to have an ambiguous effect—to shine for believers, but to seem dull and worthless to nonbelievers:

> 3. Make a list of the books that have been written by the Lord through me from the beginning up to the present time.
>
> 4. They have been written in such a way that they shine before the very eyes of those who believe in the Lord and the new revelation; but they are darkness and of no importance for those who deny those things, and who, for various external reasons, are not inclined to accept them.
>
> Experiences proving that this is the style of writing within them: 1. From the Dutch censors of books who had assembled in the spiritual world; one of them when

he had read them, said that they were of the highest merit, above every other book with the exception of the Word; but another said that he saw nothing in them but matters of a trivial kind, mere fantasies, and thus that they were to be rejected as being of no importance. 2. Likewise in England the books which have been sent to the universities, for the clergy have rejected them; 3. and by those in Göteborg, Beyer, Rosén, and others; some have indeed seen those books as mighty works of God, some nothing but trickery, and others nothing whatsoever.[23]

Because of the specific Latin style he used, then, Swedenborg can make the assertion that ends *Heaven and Hell:*

> What I have been saying in this book about heaven, the world of spirits, and hell, will be obscure to people who find no delight in knowing about spiritual truths; but it will be clear to people who do have this delight, especially to people involved in an affection for truth for its own sake—that is, people who love truth because it is true.[24]

Presumably the same applies to all of Swedenborg's theological works.

SEVEN

Swedenborg's Invitation

n the fall of 1767, three children who had come to Stockholm for their father's funeral took refuge from a sudden downpour in a covered area by the sidewalk. It happened to be part of the fence around Swedenborg's garden. The children were startled when an elderly gentleman came out in the pouring rain toward them. He invited them in to warmth and shelter, and they accepted. They apologized, asking forgiveness for being on his property, and explained the unfortunate reason for their visit to Stockholm. He replied, "That I know already; for your father has just been with me and told me that you were coming."[1]

Just as Swedenborg leaves the responsibility for salvation to the individual, so he gives his readers the responsibility for what they find. Some visitors to the garden of Swedenborg's theology are there out of curiosity, and may find beauty and order. Some who feel spiritually orphaned may also find shelter and warmth.

Appendix

Theological Works Published by Emanuel Swedenborg

The following list shows the titles adopted in the New Century Edition of the Works of Emanuel Swedenborg for the eighteen theological works published by Emanuel Swedenborg. The New Century Edition is a modern-language, scholarly translation of Emanuel Swedenborg's theological writings, published by the Swedenborg Foundation. Because there are many other translations and editions of Swedenborg's works, it is customary to refer to Swedenborg's writings by section number rather than page number; all references to Swedenborg's writings in this book follow that format.

In this list, the short title is followed by the traditional translation of the title; by the original Latin title, with its full translation; and finally by the place and date of original publication. The titles given below as theological works published by Swedenborg are generally not further referenced in this work.

❧ *Secrets of Heaven* ❧

Traditional title: *Arcana Coelestia*

Original title: *Arcana Coelestia, Quae in Scriptura Sacra, seu Verbo Domini Sunt, Detecta: . . . Una cum Mirabilibus Quae Visa Sunt in Mundo Spirituum, et in Coelo Angelorum* [A Disclosure of Secrets of Heaven Contained in Sacred Scripture, or the Word of the Lord, . . . Together with Amazing Things Seen in the World of Spirits and in the Heaven of Angels]. London: 1749–1756.

❧ *Heaven and Hell* ❧

Traditional title: *Heaven and Hell*

Original title: *De Coelo et Ejus Mirabilibus, et de Inferno, ex Auditis et Visis* [Heaven and Its Wonders and Hell: Drawn from Things Heard and Seen]. London: 1758.

❧ *New Jerusalem* ❧

Traditional title: *New Jerusalem and Its Heavenly Doctrine*

Original title: *De Nova Hierosolyma et Ejus Doctrina Coelesti: Ex Auditis e Coelo: Quibus Praemittitur Aliquid de Novo Coelo et Nova Terra* [The New Jerusalem and Its Heavenly Teaching: Drawn from Things Heard from Heaven: Preceded by a Discussion of the New Heaven and the New Earth]. London: 1758.

❧ *Last Judgment* ❧

Traditional title: *The Last Judgment*

Original title: *De Ultimo Judicio, et de Babylonia Destructa: Ita Quod Omnia, Quae in Apocalypsi Praedicta Sunt, Hodie Impleta Sunt: Ex Auditis et Visis* [The Last Judgment and Babylon Destroyed, Showing That at This Day All the Predictions of the

Book of Revelation Have Been Fulfilled: Drawn from Things Heard and Seen]. London: 1758.

⚜ *White Horse* ⚜

Traditional title: *The White Horse*

Original title: *De Equo Albo, de Quo in Apocalypsi, Cap. XIX: Et Dein de Verbo et Ejus Sensu Spirituali seu Interno, ex* Arcanis Coelestibus [The White Horse in Revelation Chapter 19, and the Word and Its Spiritual or Inner Sense (from *Secrets of Heaven*)]. London: 1758.

⚜ *Other Planets* ⚜

Traditional titles: *Earths in the Universe, Life on Other Planets, The Worlds in Space*

Original title: *De Telluribus in Mundo Nostro Solari, Quae Vocantur Planetae, et de Telluribus in Coelo Astrifero, deque Illarum Incolis, Tum de Spiritibus et Angelis Ibi: Ex Auditis et Visis* [Planets or Worlds in Our Solar System, and Worlds in the Starry Heavens, and Their Inhabitants, As Well as the Spirits and Angels There: Drawn from Things Heard and Seen]. London: 1758.

⚜ *The Lord* ⚜

Traditional title: *Doctrine of the Lord*

Original title: *Doctrina Novae Hierosolymae de Domino* [Teachings for the New Jerusalem on the Lord]. Amsterdam: 1763.

⚜ *Sacred Scripture* ⚜

Traditional title: *Doctrine of the Sacred Scripture*

Original title: *Doctrina Novae Hierosolymae de Scriptura Sacra* [Teachings for the New Jerusalem on Sacred Scripture]. Amsterdam: 1763.

⁜ *Life* ⁜

Traditional title: *Doctrine of Life*

Original title: *Doctrina Vitae pro Nova Hierosolyma ex Praeceptis Decalogi* [Teachings about Life for the New Jerusalem: Drawn from the Ten Commandments]. Amsterdam: 1763.

⁜ *Faith* ⁜

Traditional title: *Doctrine of Faith*

Original title: *Doctrina Novae Hierosolymae de Fide* [Teachings for the New Jerusalem on Faith]. Amsterdam: 1763.

⁜ *Supplements* ⁜

Traditional title: *Continuation Concerning the Last Judgment*

Original title: *Continuatio de Ultimo Judicio: Et de Mundo Spirituali* [Supplements on the Last Judgment and the Spiritual World]. Amsterdam: 1763.

⁜ *Divine Love and Wisdom* ⁜

Traditional title: *Divine Love and Wisdom*

Original title: *Sapientia Angelica de Divino Amore et de Divina Sapientia* [Angelic Wisdom about Divine Love and Wisdom]. Amsterdam: 1763.

⁜ *Divine Providence* ⁜

Traditional title: *Divine Providence*

Original title: *Sapientia Angelica de Divina Providentia* [Angelic Wisdom about Divine Providence]. Amsterdam: 1764.

⚜ *Revelation Unveiled* ⚜
Traditional title: *Apocalypse Revealed*
Original title: *Apocalypsis Revelata, in Qua Deteguntur Arcana Quae Ibi Praedicta Sunt, et Hactenus Recondita Latuerunt* [The Book of Revelation Unveiled, Uncovering the Secrets That Were Foretold There and Have Lain Hidden until Now]. Amsterdam: 1766.

⚜ *Marriage Love* ⚜
Traditional title: *Conjugial Love, Married Love*
Original title: *Delitiae Sapientiae de Amore Conjugiali: Post Quas Sequuntur Voluptates Insaniae de Amore Scortatorio* [Wisdom's Delight in Marriage Love: Followed by Insanity's Pleasure in Promiscuous Love]. Amsterdam: 1768.

⚜ *Survey* ⚜
Traditional title: *Brief Exposition*
Original title: *Summaria Expositio Doctrinae Novae Ecclesiae, Quae per Novam Hierosolymam in Apocalypsi Intelligitur* [Survey of Teachings for the New Church Meant by the New Jerusalem in the Book of Revelation]. Amsterdam: 1769.

⚜ *Soul-Body Interaction* ⚜
Traditional title: *Intercourse between the Soul and Body*
Original title: *De Commercio Animae et Corporis, Quod Creditur Fieri vel per Influxum Physicum, vel per Influxum Spiritualem, vel*

per Harmoniam Praestabilitam [Soul-Body Interaction, Believed to Occur either by a Physical Inflow, or by a Spiritual Inflow, or by a Preestablished Harmony]. London: 1769.

⚜ *True Christianity* ⚜

Traditional title: *True Christian Religion*

Original title: *Vera Christiana Religio, Continens Universam Theologiam Novae Ecclesiae a Domino apud Danielem Cap. VII:13–14, et in Apocalypsi Cap. XXI:1, 2 Praedictae* [True Christianity: Containing a Comprehensive Theology of the New Church That Was Predicted by the Lord in Daniel 7:13–14 and Revelation 21:1, 2]. Amsterdam: 1771.

Notes

Introduction

1. For descriptions of the garden, see George F. Dole
   and Robert H. Kirven, *A Scientist Explores Spirit*
   (New York: Swedenborg Foundation, 1992), 43–45;
   Olle Hjern, "Swedenborg in Stockholm," in *Emanuel
   Swedenborg: A Continuing Vision,* ed. Robin Larsen
   et al., 325–30 (New York: Swedenborg Foundation,
   1988); Cyriel Odhner Sigstedt, *The Swedenborg Epic:
   The Life and Works of Emanuel Swedenborg* (London:
   Swedenborg Society, 1981), 237–46, 312, 491–93;
   R. L. Tafel, *Documents Concerning the Life and Character
   of Emanuel Swedenborg* (London: Swedenborg Society, 1875), 1:32–33, 55–56, 390–92. The first three of
   these four sources provide drawings that reconstruct
   what Swedenborg's garden may have looked like in its
   heyday. The drawings should be treated, however, with
   some caution. They are based on eyewitness accounts,
   but follow them somewhat loosely. Furthermore, the
   accounts reflect the state of the property over a wide
   range of dates: 1752, 1921, 1867, and 1772, respectively.
   Though the description of the plants and buildings in
   this essay is based on these eyewitness testimonies,
   given the nature of that evidence and the ephemeral-
   ity of garden stock, certainty about what the garden

looked like at a given time is unobtainable now. As a further aside, it may be worth noting that Swedenborg records having seen a garden in the spiritual world in which different types of vegetation grew at the various points of the compass; see *True Christianity* 78:1. (It is customary to refer to passages in Swedenborg's works by section numbers rather than page numbers, as the former are uniform in all editions.) And finally, readers may be intrigued to know that in *True Christianity* 112 Swedenborg recounts a spiritual experience that occurred in his own garden.

Chapter 1

1. *Secrets of Heaven* 68; translation by Lisa Hyatt Cooper.
2. In an account of a memorable occurrence in the spiritual world, Swedenborg reports that an adversary described him as someone "out of the herd of the laity. He has no gown, no cap, no laurel" (*True Christianity* 137:2). These items are all trappings of advanced priestly and academic status. For a discussion of Swedenborg's accounts of memorable occurrences, see pages 59–60. (This and all other translations in this essay are my own, unless further ascription is given in the notes or bibliography.)
3. Swedenborg reports that he began having spiritual experiences in 1743 and by 1745 was in daily contact with the other world. He claims a number of times that from then on he lived in both worlds at once: see *Secrets of Heaven* Genesis 16 preface:3, 9439; *Heaven and Hell* 577:3; *Marriage Love* 1; *True Christianity* 157,

281, 695:2, 851. Nevertheless he occasionally mentions leaving his body and returning, and at one point he records a spirit's astonishment at seeing him passing in and out of visibility as he moves himself back and forth between an earthly and a spiritual state (*Marriage Love* 326). In §157 of his last work, *True Christianity*, he seems to nod to this discrepancy when he asserts that for twenty-six years he has been "in my spirit and my body at the same time, and only sometimes out of my body." Another striking instance of interaction between the two worlds can be seen in *Marriage Love* 329, in which some boys in the spiritual world follow Swedenborg home to his lodgings in the material world and comment on an insect that crawls across the page on which he is writing.

4. On the question of Swedenborg's sanity, see "The Madness Hypothesis," *The New Philosophy* 101, nos. 1 and 2 (1998).

5. Immanuel Kant, *Kant on Swedenborg: Dreams of a Spirit-Seer and Other Writings* (West Chester, PA: Swedenborg Foundation, 2002), 67–72.

6. For documentation and discussion of these three anecdotes, see Richard Smoley, "The Inner Journey of Emanuel Swedenborg," in *Emanuel Swedenborg: Essays for the New Century Edition on His Life, Work, and Impact*, ed. Jonathan S. Rose et al., 34–36 (West Chester, PA: Swedenborg Foundation, 2005); Tafel, *Documents* (London: Swedenborg Society, 1877), 2:613–66; and Sigstedt, *The Swedenborg Epic* 269–81. To these more notable events might be added a fourth:

he accurately predicted the date of his death (Tafel, *Documents*, 2:546, 567).

7. Alfred Acton, trans. and ed., *The Letters and Memorials of Emanuel Swedenborg* (Bryn Athyn, PA: Swedenborg Scientific Association, 1955), 2:749–50.

8. For other such anecdotes, see Sigstedt, *The Swedenborg Epic*, 281–86.

Chapter 2

1. See especially *Divine Providence* 27–45, 323–24, and *True Christianity* 66–67; see also *Secrets of Heaven* 6698, 9237, 9441; *Heaven and Hell* 417; *Last Judgment* 13; *Other Planets* 112; *Divine Providence* 202:1; *Marriage Love* 68:2.

2. This concept anticipates the phenomena of fractals and holograms, large and small fragments of which contain an image of the whole. See George F. Dole, "An Image of God in a Mirror," in *Emanuel Swedenborg: A Continuing Vision*, 374–81; Michael Talbot, "The Holographic Paradigm," in *Emanuel Swedenborg: A Continuing Vision*, 443–48. See also, from Swedenborg's writings, *Secrets of Heaven* 4523:2, 5115:1, 6013, 6057, 9278:3; *Heaven and Hell* 30, 57; *New Jerusalem* 47; *Divine Love and Wisdom* 251, 319–20, 323; *True Christianity* 604.

3. For other ways in which the Lord manifests himself, see *Secrets of Heaven* 1925:3–4; *Divine Providence* 96:6; *Revelation Unveiled* 465. For a lengthy treatment of the spiritual sun, see *Divine Love and Wisdom* 83–172.

4. *Heaven and Hell* 302; translation by George F. Dole. Compare *Divine Providence* 320. See also *Secrets of Heaven* 4151 and 4206, the latter of which adds that angels are more able to help those who take this objective stance. Swedenborg reports that "thousands of times" he has identified and rebuked the evil spirits who have directed a flow of evil and falsity into his mind, telling them to take it back and not to inflict it on him anymore (*Divine Providence* 290; see also *Secrets of Heaven* 6191). To spirits questioning this practice of Swedenborg's and claiming that he has no life of his own as a result, he replies that he was not alive before he began it (*Revelation Explained* [*Apocalypse Explained*] §1147:3).

5. *True Christianity* 3. These five points first appear in *Marriage Love* 82:1, and are discussed at some length there. They appear again in *Survey* 43 and 117, with an explanation at §44.

Chapter 3

1. *Last Judgment* 46 and notes; *Divine Providence* 328; *True Christianity* 760, 762, 786. For further discussion of Swedenborg's use of "the Word," see pages 27–29 and note 16 to Chapter 3 below.

2. The ancient church extended across "Assyria, Mesopotamia, Syria, Ethiopia, Arabia, Libya, Egypt, Philistia as far as Tyre and Sidon, and the whole land of Canaan on both the far and the near sides of the Jordan" (*Secrets of Heaven* 1238:2; translation by Lisa

Hyatt Cooper). To this list *Sacred Scripture* 21 adds
Chaldea and Nineveh. Elements of this early religion
later affected Greece and Rome (*Sacred Scripture* 117;
see also *Secrets of Heaven* 2762, 9011, 10177:10; *Sacred
Scripture* 26).

3. See *Divine Providence* 328:2–3. In Swedenborg's ter-
minology, the "Hebrew" church or nation refers to the
descendants of Abraham; later this group split into two,
and was known as "Judah," or the "Jewish" nation or
church; and "Israel," or the "Israelite" nation or church
(see 1 Kings 11:30–37).

4. The contents of these apparently anti-Semitic statements in Swedenborg's theological works are surpris-
ing given the general awareness in Swedenborg's day
of the long tradition of Jewish mysticism. His works
include enough counterbalancing material, however,
that scholars are divided on whether his theological
corpus as a whole is to be considered philo-Semitic or
anti-Semitic. See William Ross Woofenden and Jonathan S. Rose, "A Reader's Guide to *Secrets of Heaven*" in
Secrets of Heaven vol. 1, by Emanuel Swedenborg, trans.
Lisa Hyatt Cooper (West Chester, PA: Swedenborg
Foundation 2008), 52–55.

5. Following a Christian practice of his times, Swedenborg often used "Jehovah" as a rendering of the tetra-
grammaton, the four-letter name of God in Hebrew
Scripture that is sometimes transliterated "YHWH."
As others have done, Swedenborg relates the name
YHWH or Jehovah to the concept of being or "is-
ness"; see *True Christianity* 19:1, as well as 9:2–3.

6. For a brief overview of Swedenborg's teachings on God, with copious biblical support, see *The Lord*. See also *New Jerusalem* 280–310; these sections form a chapter on the topic that includes abundant further references to *Secrets of Heaven*. For a more extensive treatment, see the first three chapters of *True Christianity* (1–188).

7. The terms "glorify" and "glorification" are easy to misunderstand, because they each have two different meanings: to *deem* glorious or ascribe glory to, and to *render* glorious or actually transform. It is the latter meaning in which Swedenborg usually uses "glorify" and "glorification" in relation to Jesus's human nature. Swedenborg specifically defines it as rendering divine or uniting with the Divine (see *True Christianity* 2:2; see also 97, 105, 110:4, 114, 126, 128, 130:2, 154:6). Swedenborg apparently derives this usage from the Gospel of John. Although generally in the Bible the word "glorify" means to praise or extol (the first meaning just given) and Swedenborg occasionally uses the word in this sense (see *True Christianity* 16:1, 117), the Gospel of John often uses "glorify" in the second sense given above. For example, to say that the Holy Spirit had not yet come into existence because Jesus was not glorified yet (John 7:39) clearly does not mean that Jesus was not praised yet; it means that he was not yet completely transformed or rendered fully divine. For this latter usage, in addition to John 7:39 see John 12:16, 23; 13:31–32; 17:1, 5; Acts 3:13; Hebrews 5:5.

8. For Swedenborg's teachings on and experiences of the Last Judgment, see especially *Last Judgment* and

the first part of *Supplements.* More details are given throughout *Revelation Unveiled.*

9. See Daniel 2:31–35; Ovid, *Metamorphoses,* 1:89–150.

10. For the way in which Swedenborg's works relate to the Second Coming, see *True Christianity* 779 and its context.

11. See appendix, pages 67–72, for a list of these eighteen titles. Ten of the eighteen refer to the New Jerusalem or the Book of Revelation (whose last two chapters foretell the New Jerusalem).

12. On the restoration of spiritual monogamy in the new church, see *Marriage Love* 81:5 and 43. On the new church's predicted oneness with the Lord, see *Revelation Unveiled* 882–83 and *Heaven and Hell* 304. On the new church's affiliation and communication with heaven, see *Revelation Unveiled* 176–7; also see *Secrets of Heaven* 68, 1276, 1771, 1880:4, 2737, 2759:2, 2760:2, 2851:2, 5344, 5700, 5726, 8367, 8512–13, 8694:2, 8971:1, 9594, 9709, 10156:4; *Heaven and Hell* 304; *New Jerusalem* 43–44; *True Christianity* 401:7–8, 719, 846:2.

13. Translation by Lisa Hyatt Cooper. See also *Secrets of Heaven* 6377:4. For the unintelligibility of the literal meaning of many biblical passages, see *Sacred Scripture* 15.

14. *Secrets of Heaven,* an exposition of Genesis and Exodus, filled eight thick quarto volumes in the first edition, and *Revelation Unveiled,* an exposition of the Book of Revelation, filled a ninth. Yet Swedenborg presents these books as revealing only a fraction of the inner meaning (*Secrets of Heaven* 64).

15. See also Swedenborg's assertion in his preface to *Revelation Unveiled* that the Book of Revelation has nothing to do with earthly kingdoms and empires.

16. Swedenborg actually sends a mixed signal on this point. According to statements early in the theological works, books in the Protestant Old Testament that Swedenborg does not consider to be the Word are Ruth, 1 and 2 Chronicles, Ezra, Nehemiah, Esther, Job, Proverbs, Ecclesiastes, and the Song of Solomon; of the New Testament, the Word in this sense includes only the four Gospels and the Book of Revelation, not the Acts and Epistles (*Secrets of Heaven* 10325; *New Jerusalem* 266; *White Horse* 16). In his last major published theological work, however, the Acts and Epistles are included as part of the Word (*True Christianity* 158) and are referred to as such (*True Christianity* 601, 675:2). See also Acton, *The Letters and Memorials of Emanuel Swedenborg*, 2:612–13, where Swedenborg describes the Epistles as doctrinal works that provide a less direct connection with heaven but are easier to understand than the Gospels and Revelation; he asserts that they teach the importance of goodwill just as strongly as the Gospels. Swedenborg did not restore any books removed from the Catholic Bible by the Protestants, nor did he bring into his canon any other apocryphal works. He does make use, however, of what he characterizes as noncanonical works, especially Job and the Epistles. Such quoting is heaviest in *True Christianity*. He also quotes Christian creeds and other ecclesiastical documents.

17. Short chapters on each sacrament appear in *New Jerusalem* (202–22) and longer chapters in *True Christianity* (667–752). See also the account by Swedenborg of a discussion that took place in the spiritual world in *Revelation Unveiled* 224:11–13.

18. For Swedenborg's idea of usefulness as crucial to heavenly happiness, see the accounts of memorable occurrences in the spiritual realm at the beginning of *Marriage Love* (1–26). See also the chapter in *Heaven and Hell* on the work that angels do (§§387–94).

19. Wouter J. Hanegraaff, *New Age Religion and Western Culture: Esotericism in the Mirror of Secular Thought* (Albany: State University of New York Press, 1998), 424–29.

20. On the potential dangers of interacting with spirits, see *Heaven and Hell* 249 and 292. On the possibility of such interaction, see note 3 to chapter 1 and note 4 to chapter 2 above. On correspondences, see *Heaven and Hell* 87–115. On correspondences as they relate to the human form, see *Secrets of Heaven* 2987–3003, 3213–77, 3337–52, 3472–85, 3624–49, 3741–50, 3883–96, 4039–55, 4218–28, 4318–31, 4403–21, 4523–34, 4622–34, 4652–60, 4791–4806, 4931–53, 5050–62, 5171–90, 5377–96, 5552–73, 5711–27, and John Worcester, *Correspondences of the Bible: The Human Body* (West Chester, PA: Swedenborg Foundation, 2009). On memories stored in body parts, see *Heaven and Hell* 463. On inflow, also called influx, see *Soul-Body Interaction* and John F. Potts, *The Swedenborg Concordance: A Complete Work of Reference*

to the Theological Writings of Emanuel Swedenborg; Based on the Original Latin Writings of the Author (London: Swedenborg Society, 1888–1902), 3:637–71 (under "Influx"). For Swedenborg's use of gardens for connection with the spiritual world, see *Heaven and Hell* 109. For the energy or auras around human beings, animals, plants, metals, stones, and soils see *Divine Love and Wisdom* 292–93 and *Marriage Love* 171 and 224.

21. For Swedenborg's teachings on hell, see especially *Heaven and Hell* 536–88. On the relative pleasantness of one's first few hours in hell, see *Heaven and Hell* 574.

22. *True Christianity* 531; see also 614. Compare *Heaven and Hell* 356:3 and the account of a memorable occurrence in the spiritual realm in *Marriage Love* 521–22, in which an area in the woods where satyrs play is later cultivated to become a field.

23. Jonathan S. Rose, "The Ornaments in Swedenborg's Theological First Editions," *Covenant: A Journal Devoted to the Study of the Five Churches,* 1:295–96, 306.

Chapter 4

1. In addition, Swedenborg's published theological works include two statements that seem to cast aspersions on women's ability to write (*Marriage Love* 175:3; *Divine Love and Wisdom* 361; for a brief discussion of the latter, see the note by George F. Dole and Stuart Shotwell in Emanuel Swedenborg, *Divine Love and Wisdom,* trans. George F. Dole [West Chester, PA: Swedenborg Foundation, 2003], 286 n. 191); and two statements

that seem to suggest women are less rational than men and should therefore be subject to them (*Secrets of Heaven* 266; 568:2). For a discussion of the latter two passages, see Woofenden and Rose, "A Reader's Guide to *Secrets of Heaven*," 55–56.

2. Swedenborg extends the father's influence even to such apparently bodily characteristics as race when he asserts that black fathers have black children by white mothers and vice versa (*Divine Providence* 277:3). *Divine Providence* 330:1 gives a somewhat different perspective: it asserts that life comes from the Lord as heavenly Father, while earthly fathers merely supply the body, the "clothing of life." For historical background to the idea that the soul comes from the father, see Gregory R. Johnson's note on *Divine Love and Wisdom* 269 in Swedenborg, *Divine Love and Wisdom* (Swedenborg Foundation, 2003), 282 n. 146.

3. In merely illustrating rather than laying a foundation for his theology, Swedenborg here and there mentions scientific beliefs of his day that current science generally sees as unfounded or unscientific. For example, he believes in the existence of the ether, a light-conducting atmosphere more rarified than air (as for example at *Divine Love and Wisdom* 158 and *True Christianity* 30:2). He assumes the action of spontaneous generation, or abiogenesis, a process by which under certain conditions animals are formed spontaneously out of inert matter (*Divine Love and Wisdom* 342). He accepts the notion that all plants are male and

the ground is female (*True Christianity* 585), despite the contemporaneous elucidations on the two sexes in plants by Carolus Linnaeus (1707–78), Swedenborg's famous cousin-in-law (Lars Bergquist, "Linnaeus and Swedenborg," *Arcana* 3, no. 3 [1997]:23–39; Anja Hübener, "Carolus Linnaeus," in *Emanuel Swedenborg: A Continuing Vision,* 449–56). He also accepts six thousand years as the age of the world, apparently following the calculation of James Ussher (1580–1655) that the date of creation is 4004 BCE (*Secrets of Heaven* 9441; *Heaven and Hell* 417; *Other Planets* 126; *Marriage Love* 29, 39, 182:5; *True Christianity* 693:5).

4. Such references occur in *Secrets of Heaven* 908:3, 3147:10, 4750:6, 4818:2, 4825, 4832, 4865, 6561:2, 8301:5, 8588:4, 9391:19, 9942:14, 9960:18, 9962, 10033:6.

5. Such references occur in *Secrets of Heaven* 302, 788:2, 1094:2, 1850:4, 3479:3, 3881:10, 4750:6, 4865, 4911, 6963:2, 7051, 8301:6; *Supplements* 82; *Divine Providence* 182; *True Christianity* 521, 801. See also Woofenden and Rose, "A Reader's Guide to *Secrets of Heaven,*" 52–55.

6. *Secrets of Heaven* 941, *Supplements* 80, and *Secrets of Heaven* 3479:3 respectively.

7. See *Secrets of Heaven* 9237; *Heaven and Hell* 417; *Last Judgment* 13.

8. For a discussion of Swedenborg's teachings regarding life on other planets and how those teachings relate to ancient and modern views, see Allen J. Bedford, "Planets

and Perspectives: New Church Theology and the Plurality of Worlds Debate," *New Philosophy* 109, nos. 1 and 2 (2006):315–340.

Chapter 5

1. *Secrets of Heaven* 4528:3; translation by Lisa Hyatt Cooper.

2. For a thorough collection of passages on Swedenborg's persona in all his theological works, both published and unpublished, see Potts, *The Swedenborg Concordance*, 6:114–58 (under "Swedenborg").

3. *Marriage Love* 107; for a more complete discussion of this passage see Jonathan S. Rose, "Boundaries, Looks, and Style: Overlooked Aspects of Faithful Translation," *Studia Swedenborgiana* 8, no. 4 (1994):58–63.

4. Dole and Kirven, *A Scientist Explores Spirit,* 45.

5. *Secrets of Heaven* 10325; *New Jerusalem* 266. The same list is also given in *White Horse* 16. See note 16 to chapter 3 above for the books that Swedenborg excludes.

6. Tafel, *Documents,* 1:33, 56.

7. The heavenly meaning of a passage is given in *Secrets of Heaven* 2157, 4735, 5331, 10265, 10624; and in the chapter in *True Christianity* on the Ten Commandments (§§282–331). The heavenly meaning is acknowledged or discussed in *Secrets of Heaven* 9407:4; *Divine Love and Wisdom* 221; *True Christianity* 248; and here and there in *Sacred Scripture.*

8. For a threefold example of the same phenomenon, Swedenborg mentions that Christianity has three branches:

the "Greek" church (probably meaning Eastern Ortho-
dox Christianity); the Roman Catholic church; and the
Protestant or Reformed church (*True Christianity* 760).
He discusses Protestantism and Catholicism at great
length and in much detail, but makes only two brief
statements about the "Greek" church—that it long ago
separated from Roman Catholicism (*Survey* 18), and
that it believes the Holy Spirit is sent directly by God
(*True Christianity* 153, 647:3).

9. For a collection of such indications from one work
   alone, *Heaven and Hell,* see Kristin King, "Reading
   What Swedenborg's Writings Say They Cannot Say,"
   New Church Life 119:344–59, 392–410.

10. *Revelation Explained* [*Apocalypse Explained*] 152:11,
    274:3, 313:15, 1081:4. Although Swedenborg indicates
    that the meaning of the eye is a key, he elaborates well
    beyond it: he expounds the lamp, the simplicity, the
    wholeness of the body, the greatness of the darkness;
    delves into the original Greek; and even explains what
    the left and right eyes would have meant if they had
    been mentioned. (I am grateful to Kyra Hendricks for
    bringing this example to my attention.)

11. *Revelation Unveiled* 926, 961; *Marriage Love* 42, 43, 75,
    132, 137, 155b, 208, 261, 263, 267, 316, 380, 415, 444,
    461, 483; *Survey* 119; *True Christianity* 25, 76, 78, 112,
    508, 662.

12. Swedenborg's works contain a wealth of information on
    expounding Scripture, but a scattered wealth. William
    F. Pendleton, *The Science of Exposition* (Bryn Athyn,

PA: Academy of the New Church, 1915) and other resources have brought these ingredients together.

Chapter 6

1. For example, Swedenborg gives a number of quotations from poets in *The Principia; or, The First Principles of Natural Things,* trans. Augustus Clissold (Bryn Athyn, PA: Swedenborg Scientific Association, 1988), 1:387–390, 2:251–257.

2 A few surviving sources, most notably the comedies of Titus Maccius Plautus (254?–184 BCE) and Terence (Publius Terentius Afer, about 185–159? BCE), give valuable impressions of what the spoken language may have been like.

3. Hans Helander, introduction to *Ludus Heliconius and Other Latin Poems,* by Emanuel Swedenborg, ed. and trans. by Hans Helander (Uppsala: University of Uppsala, 1995), 18.

4. The volume of poetry is *Heliconian Pastime* (Swedenborg, *Ludus Heliconius and Other Latin Poems*); the poetical prose works are *Joyous Accolade* (Emanuel Swedenborg, *Festivus Applausus in Caroli XII in Pomeraniam Suam Adventum,* trans. and ed. Hans Helander [Uppsala: University of Uppsala, 1985]); and *Northern Muse* (Emanuel Swedenborg, *Camena Borea,* trans. and ed. Hans Helander [Uppsala: University of Uppsala, 1988]).

5. *The Infinite,* preface; translation by Stuart Shotwell. For a Latin version of this work, see Emanuel Sweden-

borg, *Prodromus Philosophiae Ratiocinantis de Infinito, et Causa Finali Creationis,* ed. Thomas Murray Gorman, 2nd ed. (London: Kegan Paul, Trench, 1886). For a complete translation, see Emanuel Swedenborg, *Forerunner of a Reasoned Philosophy Concerning the Infinite, the Final Cause of Creation; Also the Mechanism of the Operation of the Soul and Body,* trans. James John Garth Wilkinson, 3rd ed. (London: Swedenborg Society, 1965).

6. For Swedenborg's own lists of his theological titles, see the last page of the first edition of *Marriage Love* (Emanuel Swedenborg, *Delitiae Sapientiae de Amore Conjugiali* [Amsterdam, 1768], 328), and Acton, *Letters and Memorials of Emanuel Swedenborg,* 2:744–5.

7. Contemporary testimony comes from the Amsterdam merchant J. C. Cuno (1708–96), who knew Swedenborg late in the latter's life: "One dare not accuse Swedenborg of lack of clearness, else one would do him great injustice. He writes very simply, clearly, and understandably; indeed his relations [that is, accounts of memorable occurrences] are so circumstantial and frequently so picturesque that one could paint his narratives." J. C. Cuno, *J. C. Cuno's Memoirs on Swedenborg,* trans. Claire E. Berninger (Bryn Athyn, PA: Academy Book Room, 1947), 5. More recent testimony comes from the Neo-Latin scholar Jozef IJsewijn: "Somewhere between . . . strictly scientific Latin and literary prose we find some remarkable works of a very peculiar character, namely Swedenborg's natural, theosophical,

and moral writings written in a straightforward modern Latin." Jozef IJsewijn, *Companion to Neo-Latin Studies. Part I: History and Diffusion of Neo-Latin Literature,* 2nd ed. (Leuven: Leuven University Press, 1990), 279.

8. When Neo-Latinist scholars Margaret Benner and Emin Tengstrom give "examples of varying styles" of Swedish Neo-Latin between 1611 and 1716, they start at a low level with two texts written for "young people"; yet even these seem more elevated than Swedenborg's explanatory style. Margaret Benner and Emin Tengstrom, *On the Interpretation of Learned Neo-Latin: An Explorative Study Based on Some Texts from Sweden (1611–1716)* (Göteborg: University of Göteborg, 1977), 98–99.

9. *Ad C. Herennium de Ratione Dicendi,* trans. Harry Caplan (Cambridge: Harvard University Press, 1954), 4:8–11.

10. *Revelation Unveiled* 3; translation by George F. Dole.

11. Swedenborg's clause structures are discussed in Jonathan S. Rose, "Latin Styles of Swedenborg and His Contemporaries: Early Spadework," *The New Philosophy* 101:247–302.

12. To specify more precisely for interested Latinists: In expressing indirect discourse he moves away from the more literary method that uses accusative and infinitive toward the more conversational method that uses the conjunction *quod* with subjunctive verbs. For further details, see Alvar Erikson, "Some Observations on the Style of Swedenborg," *Classica et Mediaevalia* 9:622–8.

13. For a discussion of these various styles see Rose, "Boundaries, Looks, and Style," 49–64.

14. Rose, "The Ornaments in Swedenborg's Theological First Editions," 298, 339.

15. *Divine Providence* 340:6–7. In four cases, material that is later repeated as a memorable occurrence first appears without that label in earlier works: *Sacred Scripture* 26, 90, 102; *Faith* 42.

16. Acton, *Letters and Memorials of Emanuel Swedenborg,* 2:610, 612.

17. James Hyde, *A Bibliography of the Works of Emanuel Swedenborg, Original and Translated* (London: Swedenborg Society, 1906), entry 2195.

18. Jonathan S. Rose, "Similes in Emanuel Swedenborg's *Vera Christiana Religio* (1771)" in *Acta Conventus Neo-Latini Hafniensis* (Binghamton, NY: Medieval and Renaissance Texts & Studies, 1994), 871.

19. Rose, "Boundaries, Looks, and Style," 62–64.

20. Rose, "Similes in Emanuel Swedenborg's *Vera Christiana Religio* (1771)," 871.

21. I am grateful to Scott I. Frazier for his research on this point.

22. On the popularity of garden labyrinths in Europe in the 1600s and 1700s, see Hermann Kern, *Through the Labyrinth: Designs and Meanings over 5,000 Years* (Munich: Prestel, 2000), 247–65.

23. Emanuel Swedenborg, "Ecclesiastical History of the New Church," in *Small Theological Works and Letters of Emanuel Swedenborg,* trans. and ed. John E. Elliot (London: Swedenborg Society, 1975), 193.

24. *Heaven and Hell* 603; translation by George F. Dole. See also *Marriage Love* 533, in which mysteries like the ones revealed by Swedenborg shine like a star in the spiritual world, but become dark as they are let down into the material world.

Chapter 7

1. Sigstedt, *The Swedenborg Epic*, 334.

Bibliography

Acton, Alfred. *The Letters and Memorials of Emanuel Swedenborg.* 2 vols. Bryn Athyn, PA: Swedenborg Scientific Association, 1948–1955.

Bedford, Allen J. "Planets and Perspectives: New Church Theology and the Plurality of Worlds Debate," *New Philosophy* 109, nos. 1 and 2 (2006):315–340.

Benner, Margaret, and Emin Tengstrom. *On the Interpretation of Learned Neo-Latin: An Explorative Study Based on Some Texts from Sweden (1611–1716).* Göteborg: University of Göteborg, 1977.

Bergquist, Lars. "Linnaeus and Swedenborg." *Arcana* 3, no. 3 (1997):23–39.

Cuno, J. C. *J. C. Cuno's Memoirs on Swedenborg.* Translated by Claire E. Berninger. Bryn Athyn, PA: Academy Book Room, 1947.

Dole, George F. "An Image of God in a Mirror." In *Emanuel Swedenborg: A Continuing Vision,* edited by Robin Larsen et al. New York: Swedenborg Foundation, 1988.

Dole, George F., and Robert H. Kirven. *A Scientist Explores Spirit.* New York City and West Chester, PA: Swedenborg Foundation, 1992.

Erikson, Alvar. "Some Observations on the Style of Swedenborg." *Classica et Mediaevalia* 9 (1973):622–628.

Hanegraaff, Wouter J. *New Age Religion and Western Culture: Esotericism in the Mirror of Secular Thought.* Albany: State University of New York Press, 1998.

Helander, Hans. Introduction to *Ludus Heliconius and Other Latin Poems,* by Emanuel Swedenborg, edited and translated by Hans Helander. Uppsala: University of Uppsala, 1995.

Hjern, Olle. "Swedenborg in Stockholm." In *Emanuel Swedenborg: A Continuing Vision,* edited by Robin Larsen et al. New York: Swedenborg Foundation, 1988.

Hübener, Anja. "Carolus Linnaeus." In *Emanuel Swedenborg: A Continuing Vision,* edited by Robin Larsen et al. New York: Swedenborg Foundation, 1988.

Hyde, James. *A Bibliography of the Works of Emanuel Swedenborg, Original and Translated.* London: Swedenborg Society, 1906.

IJsewijn, Jozef. *Companion to Neo-Latin Studies. Part I: History and Diffusion of Neo-Latin Literature.* 2nd ed. Leuven, Belgium: Leuven University Press, 1990.

Kant, Immanuel. *Kant on Swedenborg: Dreams of a Spirit Seer and Other Writings.* Edited by Gregory R. Johnson and translated by Gregory R. Johnson and Glenn Alexander Magee. West Chester, PA: Swedenborg Foundation, 2002.

Kern, Hermann. *Through the Labyrinth: Designs and Meanings over 5,000 Years.* Munich: Prestel, 2000.

King, Kristin. "Reading What Swedenborg's Writings Say They Cannot Say." *New Church Life* 119 (1999):344–359, 392–410.

The New Philosophy. "The Madness Hypothesis." Vol. 101 (1998), nos. 1 and 2.

Pendleton, William F. *The Science of Exposition.* Bryn Athyn, PA: Academy of the New Church, 1915.

Potts, John F. *The Swedenborg Concordance. A Complete Work of Reference to the Theological Writings of Emanuel Swedenborg; Based on the Original Latin Writings of the Author.* 6 vols. London: Swedenborg Society, 1888–1902.

Rose, Jonathan S. "Boundaries, Looks, and Style: Overlooked Aspects of Faithful Translation." *Studia Swedenborgiana* 8, no 4 (1994):49–64.

———. "Latin Styles of Swedenborg and His Contemporaries: Early Spadework." *The New Philosophy* 101 (1998):247–302.

———. "The Ornaments in Swedenborg's Theological First Editions." *Covenant: A Journal Devoted to the Study of the Five Churches* 1 (1998):293–362.

———. "Similes in Emanuel Swedenborg's *Vera Christiana Religio* (1771)." In *Acta Conventus Neo-Latini Hafniensis.* Binghamton: Medieval & Renaissance Texts & Studies, 1994.

Sigstedt, Cyriel Odhner. *The Swedenborg Epic: The Life and Works of Emanuel Swedenborg.* London: Swedenborg Society, 1981. First edition: 1952, New York: Bookman Associates.

Smoley, Richard. "The Inner Journey of Emanuel Swedenborg." In *Emanuel Swedenborg: Essays for the New Century Edition on His Life, Work, and Impact,* edited by Jonathan S. Rose et al. West Chester, PA: Swedenborg Foundation, 2005.

Swedenborg, Emanuel. *Apocalypse Explained.* 6 vols. Translated by John C. Ager, revised by John Whitehead, and edited by William Ross Woofenden. West Chester, PA: Swedenborg Foundation, 1994–1997.

―――. *Camena Borea.* Translated and edited by Hans Helander. Uppsala: University of Uppsala, 1988.

―――. *Delitiae Sapientiae de Amore Conjugiali.* Amsterdam, 1768.

―――. *Divine Love and Wisdom.* Translated by George F. Dole. West Chester, PA: Swedenborg Foundation, 2003.

―――. *Ecclesiastical History of the New Church.* In *Small Theological Works and Letters of Emanuel Swedenborg,* translated and edited by John E. Elliot. London: Swedenborg Society, 1975.

―――. *Festivus Applausus in Caroli XII in Pomeraniam Suam Adventum.* Translated and edited by Hans Helander. Uppsala: University of Uppsala, 1985.

―――. *Forerunner of a Reasoned Philosophy Concerning the Infinite, the Final Cause of Creation; Also the Mechanism of the Operation of the Soul and Body.* 3rd ed. Translated by James John Garth Wilkinson, with an introduction by Lewis F. Hite. London: Swedenborg Society, 1965.

Revision of the 1847 edition, London: William New-bery.

———. *Ludus Heliconius and Other Latin Poems.* Translated and edited by Hans Helander. Uppsala: University of Uppsala, 1995.

———. *The Principia; or, The First Principles of Natural Things.* 2 vols. Translated by Augustus Clissold. Bryn Athyn, PA: Swedenborg Scientific Association, 1988. First edition of this translation: 1846, London: W. Newbery.

———. *Prodromus Philosophiae Ratiocinantis de Infinito, et Causa Finali Creationis.* 2nd ed. Edited by Thomas Murray Gorman. London: Kegan Paul, Trench, 1886.

Tafel, R. L. *Documents Concerning the Life and Character of Emanuel Swedenborg.* 2 vols. London: Swedenborg Society, 1875–1877.

Talbot, Michael. "The Holographic Paradigm." In *Emanuel Swedenborg: A Continuing Vision,* edited by Robin Larsen et al. New York: Swedenborg Foundation, 1988.

Woofenden, William Ross, and Jonathan S. Rose. "A Reader's Guide to *Secrets of Heaven.*" In vol. 1 of *Secrets of Heaven,* by Emanuel Swedenborg, translated by Lisa Hyatt Cooper. West Chester, PA: Swedenborg Foundation, 2008.

Worcester, John. *Correspondences of the Bible: The Human Body.* West Chester, PA: Swedenborg Foundation, 2009. First edition: 1889, Boston: Massachusetts New-Church Union.